STAGING EVENTS

STAGING EVENTS

Carolyn Soutar

The Crowood Press

First published in 2005 by
The Crowood Press Ltd
Ramsbury, Marlborough
Wiltshire SN8 2HR

www.crowood.com

British Library Cataloguing-in-Publication Data
A catalogue record for this book is available from the British Library.

ISBN 1 86126 727 4

Front cover: the Lloyds Millennium Image project, created and designed by Mike Roles; photograph by Greg Krijgsman

Typeset by Jean Cussons Typesetting, Diss, Norfolk

Printed and bound in Great Britain by Cromwell Press, Trowbridge, Wiltshire

CONTENTS

INTRODUCTION

The aim of this book is to give you, whatever your role is on an event, a step by step guide to the whole process of obtaining (or winning) and staging events. Events are produced by many organizations and at any point in your career you could find yourself responsible for organizing anything from the Christmas party to an external communications meeting. You may already be on your way to your first job on an event, but want to gain an insight into where you fit into the overall picture and any specific challenges that may await you. If you are a graduate or considering a career change, this book will help you to identify not only the role that suits your particular skills set, but the additional skills you may require.

You will see that this book focuses on the event producer, or manager, and the processes that are necessary to present a successful

Building the stage in Rio de Janeiro.

event. A successful event producer is likely to be organized, a clear communicator, perhaps creative, a good team player, a natural leader and hard working. To this list you could probably add confident with figures (or with some experience in handling budgets and spreadsheets), used to writing and able to deal with stressful situations. Whether working on a community event or for a high-profile client, the event producer must appreciate the amount of work that will be necessary to ensure that the event is perfect.

The events industry is truly a global one and you could find yourself working on events all around the world. Throughout this book, you will see references to local laws, taxes, currency, and local customs.

The technology used in workplaces or on events is constantly changing. For example, references are made to a software program, PowerPoint, which is widely used for the preparation of visual presentations. However, even if this particular program becomes obsolete in the future, some other method of preparing presentations will still be required, and issues such as ensuring that the visual presentation prepared by the speaker can be displayed using the equipment available at the venue will remain the same.

1 FINDING THAT DREAM EVENT

Imagine that you are a struggling event producer, when the phone rings and you find yourself speaking to a brand new client. The client tells you that the company's 25th anniversary is coming up, and it is to be marked with a huge celebration. There is no budget, no limit and it can be held anywhere in the world. The client is not planning to speak to any other event company regarding this event, so the project will be yours.

This really is a dream scenario. The joy of event management is that you never know what your next event will be. Whether it is a small presentation held in a hotel in the town where you are based, or an international event held in a fabulous overseas location, the processes that you need to go through in order to achieve a successful event will, by-and-large, be the same.

This chapter describes the various stages that take place before winning and staging that dream event. It is an exciting, sometimes nerve-racking and usually expensive process. It is also highly competitive. Many of the same issues will apply whether you are staging a village fete, a car launch, sporting event or if you have been volunteered to organize the office Christmas party.

Various different personnel who will work on the event are introduced during this chapter. The aim is to illustrate all the contributions that go into making an event safe, successful both financially and in terms of feedback from delegates, and enjoyable.

The events industry is about the management of expectations, both yours and the client's. This means that you or the company you work for must understand what the client wants and at all stages the client must be kept involved in the planning of the event and informed of progress.

The industry is process driven, but there is no need to be daunted by the paperwork and the systems that need to be in place. These ensure that there is a record of your event for you and your client. Having the right systems in place means that you can focus on getting the event right and enjoying it.

IDENTIFYING POTENTIAL OPPORTUNITIES

The major event companies (also called production companies) may employ a team of highly experienced sales staff to acquire new business, often referred to as the business development team. Their aim will be to make sure that a potential client is aware of their company when drawing up the list of the companies which will be taken into consideration (the pitch list). However a dedicated team is not essential and solo operators may sometimes have an advantage as they are selling themselves, rather than relying on a third

Inside a marquee.

'Once a company has decided that it wants to organize an event it should determine a budget and then call in the experts at the earliest opportunity. Most companies will want at least three quotes so be prepared to use some of the budget to fund the research that the event organizers will need to undertake. This way, event organizers can devote some real energy and time to develop really exciting plans; if they are funded they will give you a much better result without the risk that they will be out of pocket.'

Bill Vestey, Director of Public Affairs, Sony UK Ltd.

party to talk to the client on their behalf. Events are not always won by major players. The small event companies also feature on pitch lists and they too win events.

The sales team will scour the press for announcements of company flotations, mergers, launches, anniversaries: anything that might involve an external or internal communication. They will also be involved in 'cold calling', in other words phoning companies to introduce themselves in the hope that they will get that all important first meeting where the event company can present its credentials and demonstrate its experience. If the event company has teams of producers or account directors, they will keep in close contact with their previous clients, hoping to hear about any future events.

The Brief

If the client decides that it will consider you for their planned event, the next stage will be for the client to provide you with a brief for the event. This may be presented in a variety of different formats, such as, for example, the brief shown below.

> Our company is ten years old. We want to celebrate this event by holding a short meeting for 250 people, followed by a celebration meal. The second day, we will be holding morning regional seminars before people leave. We need this event to be easy to get to, with a nice hotel for all of us to stay in.

This is really a very basic brief which may well have been jotted down during a telephone conversation. More questions will be necessary in order to gain a clear understanding of what is actually wanted. The following list is not exhaustive, but it should give you an awareness of the type of information you will need in order to evaluate whether or not you wish to pitch for this event. For example, you may have a budget criterion which states that you do not pitch for events with a budget under a certain amount. You may discover that there is a pitch list of ten companies and in the face of such stiff competition you decide not to risk the money which it would cost you to pitch for the work. However, it may be worthwhile to take this risk in the hope of adding a new client to your client base.

A checklist for some of the points that you will need to clarify is given below. An in-house events organizer who has received instructions from a department within their organization will also need to consider many of the points on this checklist.

- Where is the client company based?
- How far are they prepared to travel to the event?
- What is their preferred date for this event?
- What is their budget or planned spend per delegate? (Consider whether this budget appears to be realistic.)
- What venues have been used in the past?
- What type of event has been most successful for them in previous years? Is a similar event required?
- Is entertainment required, such as a disco or themed cabaret?
- Is there any relevant background information? For example, if a company celebration is planned, can they supply any information about the culture of the company, such as the average age of the staff, male to female ratio, and so on? A start-up company with staff generally in their 20s and 30s may be looking for a very different event compared to an established company with employees covering a wider age range.
- Is your understanding of the company's brand up-to-date? At the very least, do some basic research and visit the company's website.
- Has the client regularly used a particular events company in the past? If so, it is worth trying to discover why the client is considering a change.
- How many event companies have received this brief?
- What is the deadline for the response?
- Should the presentation of your proposal, the response to this brief, be in person or by post?

The Response or the Proposal

Once you have gathered all the information you need from your client, the creative process can begin. Before you start this exciting part of the events process, make sure you have mapped out a schedule for delivery of your proposal. You may find it helpful to work this out in reverse, starting with the day on which the proposal is to be presented.

Always try to allow a 'free day' between the day when the final documents are to be produced and the day of the presentation. There is an unwritten law that the technology will let you down at a crucial moment, whether it be computers, photocopiers or whatever. It is often useful to aim to produce a draft document on a Friday, allowing time for your line manager to review it over the weekend.

A flow chart will help you plan the delivery of your proposal. Again this is not exhaustive. You may have additional deadlines, and of course, this flow chart is based on the ideal scenario of a medium length lead in.

Star Events Ltd

Event: **Date:**

Task	May 1st	May 3rd	May 4th	May 5th	May 6th	May 10th	May 11th	May 14th	May 15th	May 16th	May 16th
Brainstorm	▓										
Confirm creative proposal		▓									
Confirm budget			▓								
Brief departments				▓							
Brief suppliers, including venue search					▓						
Deadline for suppliers response						▓					
Commence creation of document, writing etc							▓				
Check document								▓			
Print document									▓		
Rehearse presentation										▓	
Presentation											▓

Document issue date:

Flow chart showing lead in time for a pitch or presentation.

You may also want to start compiling a 'contacts list' at this stage. This should include contact details for all those involved in the project, showing the client contact (including their correct title), venue details, your details, and contact details for your suppliers. It may be helpful to highlight any private telephone numbers or other contact details so that they can be removed if the list is to be publicly distributed.

Brainstorming

You have your brief, and you have added to this by asking relevant questions of your client. Now you will need to seek input from your colleagues to make this a well researched proposal and an appropriate and innovative response to the brief.

> Brainstorming: a concerted intellectual treatment of a problem by discussing spontaneous ideas about it. (dictionary definition)

Why might a brainstorming session be helpful?

- Two heads are better than one. You may be the most creative person in your company, but someone else in your office, or on your team, may have that extra idea that could tip the balance when it comes to winning the event. It is always useful to develop and refine your ideas by explaining them to an audience.
- Involving other members of the company in the development of the proposal encourages a sense of ownership and allows them to feel that they have made a contribution. This event may possibly be a major one, and if so it may be useful for your colleagues to know what it is all about, even if they are not working on it directly.
- It is useful to gain insight from a broad cross-section of individuals. For example, your client may be a large cosmetics company but no-one in your team has experience of using their products. Perhaps now is the moment to invite other members of the company in other departments to give their input into the session?
- It gives an opportunity to involve staff from all the different departments who will ultimately be involved in the project if the proposal is successful. This might be members of your creative or design team, along with the technical or production management, logistics, and videos department.

Basic brainstorming rules:

- Set a time limit for the session.
- Set out the agenda for what you want to achieve.
- Courtesy is the key: no idea is wrong, and everyone should respect the other members of the session.
- Encourage new or inexperienced members of the team to contribute. All ideas are useful, even 'Aunt Sally' contributions, in other words deliberately inappropriate ideas introduced to get everyone thinking.

At the end of this session, you should have a clear idea of where your event will be held and what your event will be. The leader of the brainstorming session should draw up a creative overview of the event outlining all the

> 'If a client wants to get the best ideas back from the organizer then they must think very carefully about the brief. They should be honest about what they want to achieve. They should tell the organizers what the budget really is otherwise they are shooting in the dark.'
>
> Simon Hambley *Acclaim!*

decisions made in the brainstorming session, and then circulate it generally to allow people to check that there are no misunderstandings.

It may also be useful to show this creative outline or event overview to suppliers to give them a clear idea of what the event is all about.

SUPPLIERS AND BUDGET

Now that the outline of the event has been sketched out, the next task is to get suppliers and other people involved. Some of the issues to consider when ensuring that your creative plan is feasible will be as follows.

- Check that a suitable venue and, if appropriate, a suitable hotel are available. You may need to make a personal visit to the planned venue to check it meets all your criteria.
- Check that any travel plans are practical.
- Check that you will have access to suitable technology or, at least, that the basic equipment necessary will be available.
- Check that your planned event will come within budget.
- Do you need to get experts to assess the suitability of the site or venue? You may have to do this for an outdoor event on a green-field site, or your insurance cover may require you to do a risk assessment of the site or venue. You may need to involve experts where you are planning a permanent installation of an exhibition or similar project, to ensure that you will comply with any planning laws or building regulations.

Your first challenge will be dividing the budget for your pitch between the various departments that may be involved. For example, this may cover the following:

- Logistics: travel, venue, delegate registration and perhaps entertainment. Logistics can also be a creative department, as they often have to devise entertainment and creative schedules for times when the delegates are not in a presentation, but are out on a city tour, or a ride and drive.
- Technical: design, lights, staging, and all other technical equipment.
- Video: if videos are part of your proposal, a budget will be needed.
- Print and design: you may wish to arrange for the preparation of invitations or handouts, signage or general branding of the event, CD-roms for the delegates, and so on.

You may need to ask the accounts department to raise an purchase order to pay for the pitch, or you may want to keep the accounts department aware of your plans so that it has advance warning of what you will require.

Once you have successfully allocated the budget to the various departments, you will need to contact the suppliers and ask them for quotes which you can incorporate into your proposal. Make sure they have a copy of the outline of the event. It may be company policy to gather in several quotes from suppliers and run a mini-tendering process, where even at this proposal stage you ask potential suppliers to pitch to you to win the work, prior to you presenting to your client. As with your presentation to your client who wants the event, the winner need not necessarily be the cheapest quote as there will always be other additional factors to consider.

After briefing the potential suppliers, emphasize the deadline by which you will need their quote, and agree with them how they are to respond, whether by post, telephone, or otherwise. Before proceeding too far, check that the suppliers are happy that the budget available is realistic. It will also be important to ask whether they expect to be busy around the date when the event is planned, especially if you have requested specific equipment or

13

> 'The choice of event organizers will always be difficult and it is worth putting some effort in to finding the right one. The best, of course, is word of mouth referral. Make sure you ask all the difficult questions – did the event come in on budget? Was it on time? Were all the sub-contractors reliable? Did the visitors to the event enjoy themselves? Were the event organizers easy to deal with? What did not work or went wrong (something certainly will have done!)?'
>
> *Bill Vestey, Director of Public Affairs,*
> *Sony UK Ltd.*

operators. This stage may be followed by a short lull while the suppliers prepare their quotes.

At this point, it may be useful to start to collect information that will be needed to create the presentation document and anything else that you may wish to take to the presentation such as mood boards, a story board for the event and so on. The client may be willing to supply a copy of its logo for your presentation document and there may be other relevant items, such as photos of the new product, which you may wish to request.

> 'The contracting company should establish a small task group who have full delegated responsibility for making the event happen. Once the event organizers are employed there is nothing more depressing than slow decision making while the company is waiting for the MD or some other senior executive to make final decisions.'
>
> *Bill Vestey, Director of Public Affairs,*
> *Sony UK Ltd.*

As quotes are received from suppliers, a 'reality check' will be required on the overall spend budget. This is a difficult process and you must decide what takes priority, whether that is travel, entertainment, or any other aspect of the event. Of course, health and safety issues will take precedence over everything else.

The budget can be presented in various different ways. Some clients like to see clear actual costs: 'actual' meaning that there is no mark-up or profit when costs from suppliers are quoted, and the fee that you will charge is shown separately.

Do not forget to include costs for time worked by the in-house permanent members of staff. You may find it useful to create a new flow chart, again starting from the event and working backwards. If you are planning to supply staff for a three-day event, with a load-in day for setting up the staging, lights etc, and the event is to be held at the other end of the country, you will need to factor in staff costs for five days' work. It is very useful to go through this process, as your client may well want an overview of how you arrived at your overall fee. Other support staff may also be needed: check with all the departments to make sure that nothing has been overlooked.

Taking the producer as an example:

- Proposal shows ten days for working to the presentation stage.
- The flow chart shows a requirement of four days work per month: this is based on preparation for a monthly meeting with the client, the meeting itself and any follow up days.

Now you need to total the days and work out the daily rates for all members of staff. Remember, that this is just a chart for 'office staff', not all the other people who will be in the various departmental budgets. Usually

Star Events Ltd

Event: Date:

Days worked	Proposal	May	June	July	August	Sept.	Oct	Nov	Dec	Pre-production	Build	Event	Wrap
Exec Producer	5	1	1	1	0	1	1	1	1	3	1	4	2
Producer	10	4	4	4	2	4	4	4	4	7	4	4	6
Project Co-ordinator	10	4	4	4	2	4	4	4	4	7	0	0	6
Technical Manager	10	4	4	4	2	4	4	4	4	7	5	5	4
Design	6	1	1	1	0	0	0	0	0	0	0	0	0
Creative Director	5	1	1	1	0	1	1	1	1	1	0	3	0
Account Director	3	2	2	2	0	2	2	2	2	2	0	3	2
Admin support	10	4	4	4	2	2	2	2	2	4	0	0	2
Logistics HOD	10	4	4	4	2	4	4	4	4	7	3	4	6
Video HOD	10	2	2	2	2	2	2	10	10	3	0	0	2
Other	5	2	2	2	2	2	2	2	2	2	2	2	2

Document issue date:

'Days worked' chart for use when preparing a budget.

'time worked' is the first part of the budget to be trimmed if money is tight. However you should always be careful not to lose days that you know will be worked.

You may be required to produce timesheets to show time worked, travel time and other items related to your job, and clients may require you to submit weekly or monthly timesheets. Even if your client does not wish to see timesheets, your own company's accounts department may ask you to prepare timesheets in any case.

Star Events Ltd

Event: **Date:**

NAME:		Week Ending: / /1999 Entered: / /1999								
CLIENT	JOB NUMBER	SAT	SUN	MON	TUE	WED	THU	FRI	**TOTAL**	
1										
2										
3										
4										
5										
6										
7										
8										
9										
10										
11										
12										
13										
14										

50% CHARGEABLE : TRAVEL TO/FROM CLIENT and PITCH

1										
2										
3										
4										

OTHER % CHARGEABLE (please specify)

1										
2										
3										

NON-CHARGEABLE

	SAT	SUN	MON	TUE	WED	THU	FRI	TOTAL	
BANK HOLIDAYS									
HOLIDAYS									
HEALTH									
INTER-OFFICE TRAVEL									
EXISTING CLIENT DEVELOPMENT									
NEW BUSINESS									
SPECIFIC CRICKET ADMIN									
OTHER (please specify)									
TOTAL NON-CHARGEABLE									
TOTAL HOURS									

Document issue date:

A sample time sheet.

Holidays

Watch out for public or national holidays on your event days and advise your client on the impact they may have on the event, travel, additional pay for local crew, and so on. Remember that many staff members will be on holiday during August.

Do not forget to take account of any local taxes, especially if the event is to be held overseas, as this may prove crucial to the budget. Make sure that your proposal clearly states whether these are included or excluded in the figures quoted to the client. If appropriate, check exchange rates for foreign currencies and state these clearly in the proposal document.

The figure shows a sample video budget as an overview or front page. Usually, detailed

Star Events Ltd

Event: **Date:**

VIDEO BUDGET		ESTIMATED COSTINGS £	
VIDEO POST PRODUCTION	Transfers		
	Graphics		
	Off-line edit		
	On-line edit		
AUDIO POST PRODUCTION	Post production		
	Royalty/music fees		
MISCELLANEOUS	Transport		
	Miscellaneous		
PRODUCTION EXPENSES	PDs/subsistence		
	Hotels		
	Travel		
SUB TOTAL	Net external costs		
CONTINGENCY	Contingency charge @ 5%		
SUB TOTAL	Total external costs		
HANDLING/ ADMINISTRATION	Handling charge @ 10%		
TOTAL COSTS	Total external costs		
CREATIVE FEES & PM	Fees	Hours @ £	
TOTAL ESTIMATED COSTING		£	

Document issue date:

Sample video budget.

pages behind this will show all the various sections that make up the main items.

Income-Based Events

If you are working with a client or promoter on an income-based event, you will need to assess the following:

- Capacity of venue. How many people can sit or stand to view your event? Who will be paying?
- What will the ticket prices be?
- Concessions. For example will family tickets be available?
- Remember to allow for additional costs such as advertising, design and printing of tickets, and any public relations (PR) required.
- Will there be any additional income from programme sales, food sales or other sales on site?

When you have estimated the above items, you can see what your break-even figure will be. This can be done by simply calculating your total costs divided by the income generated by ticket sales. Having done this, you may wish to adjust your ticket prices accordingly. Break-even figures may vary from as low as possible to over 60% (in other words, you will need to sell 60% of your capacity in order to break even). You and your client will have to decide what will be an acceptable break-even figure.

You should never include intangibles. Sponsorship, for example, should always be shown as a zero on your budget as it is unlikely that, at the proposal stage of an event, any sponsorship money will have been promised. When asking for sponsorship, remember that the sponsor may actually spend at least double the amount that they are giving to the event, on their own advertising, print costs for any leaflets they distribute, hospitality for their guests and so on. This may help to explain the

> 'When doing a fundraising event, make sure that all sponsors get the benefits that have been promised to them. If a sponsor is not happy with the effort made, they will be unwilling to help an organization again. It is easier to retain a sponsor than start the search all over again. It is also important for the sponsor to know what their money is going towards. If they feel their funds are being misused or used in a manner they don't approve of they may revoke their sponsorship.'
>
> *Kerry Peavey, Freelance Sports Events Organizer, Texas, USA*

reason why they might appear to be less than generous in the sponsorship offered.

If you wish to include sales of programmes in your budget, a useful rule of thumb is to estimate that 30% of your audience (that is, 1 in 3 of those attending the event) may purchase programmes. Do not include income from merchandizing as this again is unknown, unless, of course, it is a repeat event when you will be able to include a suitable estimated figure drawn from previous experience.

Unless you are selling hospitality packages, for example marquees that can be pre-booked for an inclusive price, you should not include hospitality in these figures. If your company or logistics or catering company are providing the corporate hospitality, then the same budget process calculating a break-even figure will need to be carried out.

Additional costs for an income-based event will include printing and designing for programmes, any costs involved in providing seating, tickets, staff to cover ticket sales and ushers, stewards and so on.

THE PAPER TRAIL

Once the budget has been checked, completed and approved as necessary within your company, this can be used as the basis for a checklist for the whole event. This checklist can also serve as an agenda for internal production or status meetings. If the client is providing a particular element of the event, note this on the checklist, and again, this can be used as an agenda point at client meetings.

This paper-trail that you are creating will form the backbone for your event file or 'job bag'. By maintaining clear records, if your client has a query at any stage you should be able to demonstrate how, when, why and by whom decisions were made.

So far your file should contain:

- List of names and addresses for all contacts.
- The brief.
- Flow chart.
- Days worked (for the budget).
- Time sheets (again, part of the budget and on-going work).
- Outline for your proposal.
- Budget.

Remember that attention to detail is crucial, as for all your documents and work. It is something that all clients will notice and gives confidence in your ability.

The checklist shown is essentially just an edited budget, with sub-headings inserted. This list is a suggestion for an indoor event and there may be some items to add when organizing an outdoor event.

THE PROPOSAL DOCUMENT

The proposal document, be it a few sheets of A4 paper or a full-colour document, bound

---

Sample Checklist for an Indoor Event

A.V. equipment	Delegate presents	Production kit or office box, stationery
A.V. staff	Designer	
Auto-Q or teleprompt	Disco	Pyrotechnical staff
Band	Event doctor (if necessary)	Running orders for crew (list of what is to happen on stage in order)
Band catering	Event photographer	
Band dressing rooms	Exhibition	
Break-out sessions	Fees	Scripts for speakers
Cabaret	Flowers, dressing	Security passes
Camera crew	Ground staff (such as interpreters, local knowledge)	Set
Car cleaners		Show call
Car drivers		Signage
Cleaners	Insurance	Simultaneous translators/interpreters
Client hotel	Limos, taxis	
Costumes and props (as requested by specific speakers)	Lighting crew	Sound
	Lighting equipment	Sound crew
	Logistics staff	Speaker's dressing rooms
Crew accommodation	Music (walk in, presentations)	Stage crew
Crew catering		Travel
Crew uniform	Photos of event	Venue
Delegate badges, registration	Print, invitations, maps	Video crew
	Prizes, awards	Videos

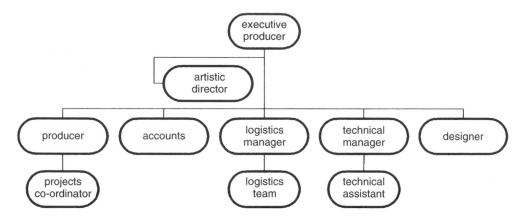

Organization chart for proposal stage.

and supported by designs, has to be as good as it possibly can be.

Obviously presentation documents will vary widely, but a guide to what could sensibly be contained in your document is given below. The figure shows a basic diagram illustrating how the various people work together on a proposal document. Other people may also be involved, for instance copywriters or 'word-smiths'.

- Introduction: usually this is a brief note stating that you are pleased to be asked to present to the company.
- The brief: a summary of your understanding of what the client wants.
- The response to the brief: a summary what you are proposing to create for the client.
- The event: a day-by-day breakdown of what will happen. The suggested venue, hotels and, if appropriate, country will be in this section. Travel arrangements and other entertainment, such as city tours and similar events, will also be included here.
- Designs: showing everything from the stage designs to print designs.
- The team for the event, giving names, titles and a brief background to the event team.

You may want to include details of suppliers and why they have been chosen.

- 'How we work': this gives an opportunity to set out how you would like to work in the period leading up to the event covering issues such as meetings, who will be the point of contact for the client, reports, and so on.
- The budget: a summary of the budget should appear on the front page, showing the cost of staging the event, as this will be the first thing that the client wishes to see. It is traditional that the budget itself should be the penultimate section of the document.
- Your company's terms and conditions: including the company's mission statement (what your company stands for, in effect, its way of working). If appropriate, information on insurance cover and anything else that you would like the client to be aware of, such as any awards won, should be included here.

When you describe what the delegates will experience, try to describe in words exactly what they will see as they walk into the event venue. Some people find it difficult to 'read' a design or a plan, so do not hesitate to spell it out. An example might be:

'Day one

12.30. The Opening Presentation

As you walk in to the Bombay suite, you will see a wide blue stage set out at the end of the room. There will be a subtle lighting state 'up' for the walk-in of the delegates. Your theme music of Vivaldi's flute concertos will be played for the walk-in. Walking past blue conference chairs, you will see a screen to the right of the stage, with the company logo set on the 'flats' and lit, on either side of the screen.

The carpet on the stage will be navy blue. The lectern, on stage left, is acrylic, to allow an unobstructed view of the speaker. To either side of the lectern will be the auto-Q or teleprompt glasses. On the floor on either side of the lectern, covered in blue carpet, will be the hoods for the comfort monitors (i.e. the monitors that show the speaker what is being displayed on the screen behind).

On the far right will be a conversation area, set with two smart but inviting sofas and a small table set with microphones. The carpet on this side of the stage will be a splash of colour, in cream and red to change the focus for the audience.

There will be two sets of steps for speakers to get on to the stage, depending where they are seated in the audience....'

This may seem very detailed, but it should leave no room for misunderstanding. An additional bonus is that if the proposal document is passed to other members of the company who have missed your presentation, even without access to your story boards or mood boards they will be given a clear view of the event.

Confidentiality

If you are about to join a large pitch list, you may need to check that your suppliers are not working for other event companies, or any other competitor. It is worth discussing whether a confidentiality agreement is worth drawing up to protect you and your ideas.

The description of the rest of the event should be equally detailed, telling the client what happens to their delegates every step of the way, covering issues such as checking in to the hotel, registering for their delegate badge, coffee breaks, and any special instructions for the gala dinner.

Your presentation must be well designed and give you the best chance possible (within the limits of your budget for pitching) of appearing memorable, clear and creative at the presentation.

THE PRESENTATION DAY

With your presentation document finalized, all your story boards or mood boards completed, and everything checked and double checked, you are ready for the presentation day.

'Never promise something that you either have no idea how you can achieve it or have no idea how much it will cost. It may be outside your skill-set. You are only human, and saying to a client that you "will get back to them," will gain you respect and time and ensure that all expectations are met, and that your company is paid for the event with no shadow of disappointment or litigation.'

Andrew Killian,
Freelance Stage Manager, UK

When you look back at the stages that you have been through to get to the presentation, you will appreciate that this can be a very expensive process. Even for a one-man company, taking account of the hours of work necessary to put together this document, there will have been a significant amount of money invested. With this investment at stake, it will be vitally important to check all the basics before making your presentation to the client.

- Who will introduce your team and start the presentation?
- Will different sections be presented by different team members?
- Will you hand out the documents before or after the presentation? If people are reading, they are generally not listening, but you should talk this through with your colleagues.
- Do you want to separate the budget, so that you can hand a copy to the client when you get to it?
- Will you leave your story boards or mood boards with the client, and if so, do you have a spare set available?
- What will the members of your team wear? This may seem basic, but different clients have different cultures, and your everyday office wear may not be theirs. It will be important for all members of your team to follow the same dress code, to present a unified impression.

The next stage will be to arrange for a rehearsal. As a rule of thumb, allow for a rehearsal time which is two-and-a-half times longer than the planned duration of your presentation. This rehearsal is crucial. Even though you may have always been a performer at heart, the other members of your team may need more encouragement. Remember that to some people even standing up in front of an audience and saying their name is anathema.

Gather all of your team in a quiet room, and discuss the presentation starting from the moment that you enter the room, including details such as where you will all sit and where you will place the various 'props', mood boards and so on. Remember to tell everyone to smile before they start speaking, as this will endear them to whoever is watching them, and crucially, it will give them confidence.

Hopefully, your presentation will be a great success. You will have had a good discussion with your client about the creative elements and cost, and you will have remembered to ask them when a decision is likely to be made.

It is possible that you may be asked to present for a second time. For a large event, there may well be a short list of potential event companies. You might be asked to look at some of your proposal again or, in very rare circumstances, you may need to create a new proposal from scratch. If you are to present for a second time, the same rules apply to rehearsals

'If you have managed to find that elusive "star" for your event and they are in your proposal, remember to explain clearly to your client the following; you probably have only done an availability and interest check and this does not guarantee that they will actually be available to do the event. If there is a long space of time between the information request and you winning the event anything might have happened to change their availability. You should explain too, that until money changes hands between the various parties, you could lose them to other people. Because they are named in your proposal is not a guarantee that the client will have them at the event.'

Andrew Killian,
Freelance Stage Manager, UK

as before. You must warm up your team again. It could be a few weeks since the first presentation and there may well be changes to be made.

WINNING THE EVENT

It's time for celebration. After your successful presentation, you have beaten all the competition and have won the event. Depending on your company's accounting or contracting process, at this point you may need to do no more than raise an invoice to the client, or there may be a full contract to draw up. When this is received, work can start.

Whether you have been successful or not, it is very useful to ask the client for feedback on your presentation, possibly by sending them an evaluation form. You might ask the client to comment on your presentation, appearance, language, clarity, response to the brief and speed of communication.

Do not forget to let everyone who worked on the pitch know about its success. Word of mouth amongst your colleagues and competition is good PR for your company. If it is appropriate and the client approves, you might consider issuing a press release to the relevant industry press.

To recap, your event file should now include:

- Contact sheet.
- The brief.

The view over the Lagao in Rio before the stage was built.

Rehearsing the dancers for an opening ceremony.

- Flow chart for presentation lead-in.
- Days worked (for the budget).
- Time sheets (again part of the budget and on-going work).
- Outline for your proposal.
- Budget.
- Completed proposal, designs etc.
- Copy of invoice to client or confirmation from client of event won.
- Client feedback form.

WORKSHOP IDEAS

There are many down times or lulls during the events seasons and gathering your team for workshops can prove very constructive. If any of the processes described earlier in this chapter are new to you or your team, you might wish to try the following exercises or workshops.

Brainstorming

Brainstorming may not be part of your company's day-to-day routine. If producers or managers are used to creating their own events they may not have a lot of experience of brainstorming. You may want to use as an example an existing event or ask the team members to create a fictional event for an existing client.

To make this exercise realistic you should:

- Create a basic brief: for example a celebration party to be held indoors.
- Work out a delivery time for your team's response or a time limit for the discussion.
- If you have a wide range of experience within your team, consider allocating team members to groups in order to ensure that the novices do not feel overwhelmed.
- Talk the team members through all the aspects of the brief, and make sure everyone remembers the basic rules: courtesy and to be aware that ostensibly no idea is a bad one.

Budgets

It is possible to gain valuable experience of working with a spreadsheet merely by working on your own home or household budget. As the software available becomes more and more sophisticated it is unlikely that you will ever have to create a budget from scratch.

Presentation Training

If your brainstorming has gone well then it would be useful to get the team leader of each discussion group to gain experience by presenting the results to the other groups. A presentation trainer may bring in fresh ideas, expertise and encouragement.

2 GETTING STARTED

You have won that elusive event and now the production process will begin in earnest.

The date of the event may be months away, giving ample time to prepare, but more often than not you may find yourself planning an event that is to be held in just a few weeks' time. This start-up period is your chance to build a relationship with your client and to deal with any issues that have arisen since the acceptance of the proposal. You will also need to confirm staff, suppliers and venue.

REVISITING THE PROPOSAL

The period after winning a pitch can bring a touch of *déjà vu*. You are about to review your proposal and meet with the client for feedback before proceeding any further. The client may have chosen your company because they liked you not your ideas. Watching your competitors' presentations may have refined the client's views on what is wanted, and you may be asked to incorporate these changes into your proposal.

Even if your client is happy with every single detail of your proposal, there still may be hurdles to address. For example, you will have to rapidly re-check the availability of venues, transport, guest speakers or performers. If some time has passed between pitching for the event and conformation that you have won, hotel rooms, for example, may no longer be available.

Here are some of the immediate steps that you need to take on winning that event.

Choosing the correct suppliers

Always make sure that the suppliers you speak to have the credentials for the specific job you are asking them to do or quote for. For example, if the event is a car-launch and you have planned a big reveal with pyrotechnics going off around the cars, check that the supplier which is to organize the display has relevant experience, appropriate insurance, has a well proven risk assessment plan and can provide references.

- Ensure that you have confirmation that your client has asked you to organize the event, either shown as a written full contract or by supplying a purchase order. Your company may have a system whereby your own internal job number is assigned to this event.
- A meeting with your client is essential to formalize what the event will be and how closely the client would like to follow your proposal.
- At this meeting, you will also need to find out the true budget for the event, published or otherwise. This may alter your ideas considerably.
- You need to confirm who will be your main point of contact with the client. Ideally your contact will be a decision maker with purchasing power.

- Check with your main point of contact (p.o.c.) how frequently status meetings will be required. Would separate meetings with your logistics department to discuss travel requirements be preferred?
- What would be your client's preferred method of accounting? Would the client wish to deal with your finance director direct, or with the producer or account director?
- Agree the date of your next meeting. This meeting will be the start of the sign-off process on the creative, the budget and any other major elements in your proposal.
- You will also need to check that all the other elements included in your proposal are available, such as specialist equipment, new technology, lighting designer and 3D designer.

This first meeting after you have won the event is crucial to building a good relationship with

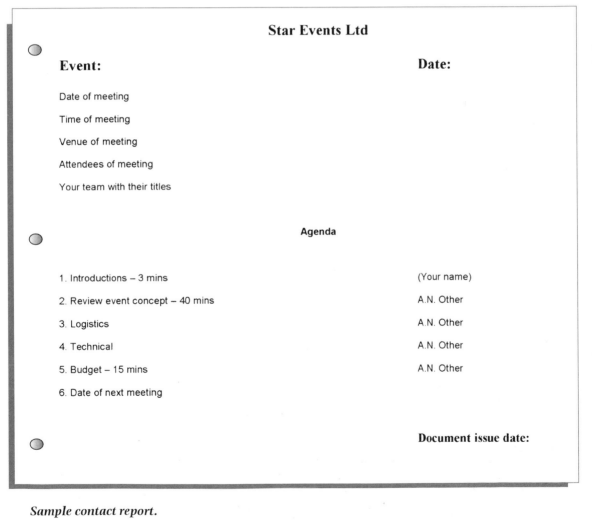

Star Events Ltd

Event: **Date:**

Date of meeting

Time of meeting

Venue of meeting

Attendees of meeting

Your team with their titles

Agenda

1. Introductions – 3 mins   (Your name)

2. Review event concept – 40 mins   A.N. Other

3. Logistics   A.N. Other

4. Technical   A.N. Other

5. Budget – 15 mins   A.N. Other

6. Date of next meeting

Document issue date:

Sample contact report.

'Make sure that there is a full and exhaustive contract between the company and the event organizers so that both sides know exactly what is expected of each other.'

Bill Vestey, Director of Public Affairs,
Sony UK Ltd.

your client. You have been given a position of trust: after all, you will be spending money on their behalf, and no matter how grand or small the spend is on this event you need to show your client that you are a clear communicator.

RECORDKEEPING

Client Contact Report

In this book, the record kept of contact with the client will be referred to as the 'client contact report'. This will be one of the documents used most over the days, weeks or months leading up to your event. You will see that the model document has an agenda attached to it. As with all meetings, check with all the various players what they will need to say or present at the meeting and how much time you should allow for their contributions.

Always set a time limit for each agenda point. Over time, you will be able to refine these time estimates and allow for people to join as and when they are required for the meeting. If the majority of the meeting is spent discussing how one particular set of delegates are going to fund the trip and their method of travel, it will be pointless for your designer and technical team to sit through the entire meeting.

A fair amount of your client meetings will be dealing with 'sign off' from the client. This covers a variety of items and could include everything from the design of the invitations to the prices charged at the bar. Keeping on top of this particular process will be a major

responsibility, but it is vital if you are to retain the continued confidence of your client.

Flow Charts Showing Progress

You will need to schedule regular team production meetings. These offer an opportunity to keep members of the event team informed of what the client has agreed and to address any issues that have arisen. You will need the input of the various heads of departments for feedback on delivery times and their opinions on the client sign-offs.

A second flow-chart will be useful to help you to do this. It is advisable to prepare the original on paper, which is secure and permanent, and also to put key dates on a wipe board as a visual reminder to the team during meetings. The flow chart will help you focus on the whole event without it seeming overpowering. You may want to transfer the key dates to your diary and give your team a reminder a few days ahead of important meetings or delivery dates.

You will find that your flow chart and your budget are your main points of reference and will need to be close to hand throughout the whole process. The more you refer to them the more familiar they will become and you will be able to keep your client and superiors up-to-date at all times. The flow of information (including clear, accurate and relevant details), will help to maintain a positive relationship with your client.

Telephone logs

You may want to create a telephone log to keep records of conversations with clients and suppliers, with dates and times and any decisions made or queries raised so that you have an accurate log of work which took place outside the context of a meeting. In some companies and organizations this is normal practice and in the United Kingdom also forms part of a quality standard.

Star Events Ltd

Event: Date:

Event title	Jan	Feb	March	April	May	June	July	August	Sept	Sept	Sept
Event sign off	▓										
Confirmation budget		▓									
Confirm design			▓								
Brief departments				▓							
Brief suppliers, including venue search					▓						
Deadline for suppliers response						▓					
Contract, confirm all suppliers							▓				
Check all sign offs, print design videos etc								▓			
Client rehearsals, script content development									▓		
Load in										▓	
Show											▓

Document issue date:

Flow chart showing lead in to event.

Idiot's List and Day File

During the 1970s, the stage management at the English National Opera developed a checklist for running operas 'blind'. These could be used if you had to stand in for a missing colleague at the last moment, and you had no previous experience of the production. Called 'Idiot's lists', these lists told a person where to be at what moment, how long they had between each cue and gave a very detailed description of what they had to look for and where to find it, for example precisely which chair out of the 20 or so that were in the wings, was the exact chair that should be handed to the singer.

Most events will not require you to keep such detailed information, but by following certain standard procedures you can help your colleagues to cope if an emergency arises while you are away from the office. Again, some companies follow these procedures as standard custom and practice. A day file in date order, containing an additional copy of your work each day, will help anyone trying to answer your calls or discover what stage planning of the event has reached. Although it may appear to be just another layer of paperwork, if you are away from your desk and your colleagues are faced with an array of files of correspondence, all arranged in subject order, they may struggle to locate the necessary information. They may find the day file is invaluable as a quick reference.

Action Lists

Action lists can be very useful and when used in addition to your client contact reports or client meeting reports they can help to focus your attention on any areas that need to be looked at.

You may, of course, want to adapt the wording of the model given in the figure to suit your event. If you are working on a large outdoor event, involving many sectors of the community and emergency services, action lists such as the one illustrated help close any holes that may otherwise not be spotted for some time,

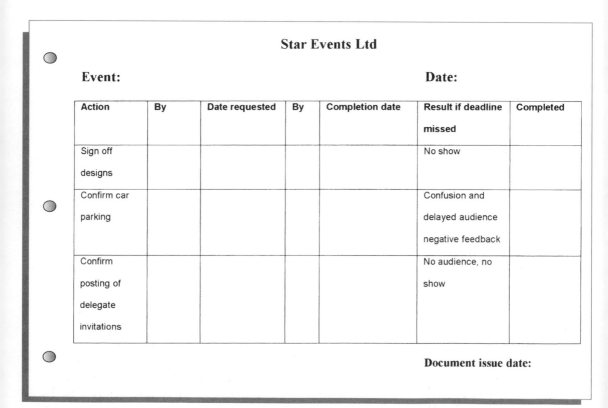

Star Events Ltd

Event: Date:

Action	By	Date requested	By	Completion date	Result if deadline missed	Completed
Sign off designs					No show	
Confirm car parking					Confusion and delayed audience negative feedback	
Confirm posting of delegate invitations					No audience, no show	

Document issue date:

Sample action list.

Star Events Ltd

Purchase Order

Event: **Date:**

Purchase Order Number   **Date**

For Services

As technical manager 36 days @ £xxx

(15 in office, 15 on site, 6 travelling)

Agreed expenses: 1 x return train fare to airport

All hotels and other travelling expenses are included

Catering on site included

Other information : Show blacks to be worn.

Signed

For Star Events

Accounts

Document issue date:

Sample purchase order.

especially if your main meetings are bi-monthly.

Of course, even at the start of the production process, your real action list will be much longer than the example shown. If you have identified that there is an area which is not on track you may find it useful to distribute copies of the action list. It can be a very effective wake-up call for those concerned to see a 'no show' marked by one of their tasks, be they client, supplier or one of your own team.

Client Sign-off Forms

If you are co-ordinating a large event and want confirmation from members of your team that the elements in their control have been cleared by your client, then you may want to use client sign-off forms in addition to the action lists. These forms should be signed and dated by your client to state what has been approved, including information on costs and so on. However, you may still want to use the contact reports to keep a record of any decisions that are made.

'Logistics budget: being responsible for your own section of an event budget is of paramount important. Having more than a rudimentary understanding of spreadsheets, too, is vital – at the end of the day, you will need to reconcile your own part of the budget and, hopefully, come out if not in profit, then having broken even.'

Emma Chesters,
Freelance Logistics Manager, UK

Purchase Orders

If you will be engaging freelance staff, you will need to issue purchase orders negotiating their terms, their rates of pay, travel and expenses. You will also need to make sure that they will be available at the time required.

The exact terms can be tricky to assess for both parties. If you are only employing a freelancer for two days per month, it can only be expected that the freelancer will take on additional contracts – but there is an unwritten rule stating if they are ever on site at an another event and unobtainable even by phone, you will need them on that exact day. Flexibility will be required on all sides.

Purchase orders are commonly used instead of letters of agreement or contracts with all types of suppliers. The terms and conditions imposed by your company are usually set out on the reverse of the purchase order. A purchase order is a contract between you and your supplier, confirming what they are supplying, the date, time, venue and any special instructions. They are commonly issued in triplicate, allowing one copy to be retained for your records, one copy for the supplier to sign and return, and one copy for the supplier to keep for their own records. As you will see in the example shown on page 31, crucially, you are also confirming the cost and any schedule of payments. The supplier will quote the purchase order number on their invoice to you which will be crucial when you come to reconcile the budget after the event.

Product Change Notice

A vital document will be the product change notice (PCN). Occasionally, you will need a product change notice as proof that the client has given authority to depart from the original agreement: usually because an unexpected expense has arisen. An additional spend, possibly an urgent cost that has come up late at night, is easily forgotten and, of course, at short notice it may not be easy to find the right person to sign your hastily produced product change notice.

You will notice that it says 'additional cost' on the example product change notice shown in the figure. You may well have an idea of what the additional spend will be, but to get the exact amount confirmed by the supplier or the venue may prove difficult. If you do not arrange for the product change notice to be signed by the client, you will run the risk of the additional expense coming out of your profit margin. Do not forget to ensure that all the relevant parties have a copy for their records.

Star Events Ltd

Product Change Notice

Event: **Date:**

Venue:

Job Number:

Client:

| **Change to original order:** | Additional catering for cabaret act and backstage refreshments in addition to their rider. | **Additional cost:** |
| | Reason: delay to their flight, lost luggage and loss of sound check time TLC! | |

Event producer: **Client signature and their title:**

Document issue date:

Sample product change notice.

Summary

To recap, you should by now have the following in place:

- A signed off event with venue, creative and any other basic issues, dates, guest speakers, and so on decided.
- A signed off budget.
- Your team 'contracted' with purchase orders issued to freelance staff as necessary.
- Records of any meetings with your client and your team.

EXHIBITIONS

You may be asked to organize an exhibition which will run alongside the main event. Whether the exhibitors are part of the client company or are external, you will need to provide them with certain basic information:

- The size of their pod, or display area, in other words the 'footprint' that they can use.
- Power supply.
- Height restrictions.

33

- Weight loading restrictions (for example if the stand has a false floor).
- Build time allowed.
- Basic schedule.
- Additional costs: power, labour, entertaining.
- Minimum and maximum number of staff.
- Any restrictions on the size of mountings or advertising boards.

They should also be given any other relevant information such as restrictions regarding fire regulations, health and safety requirements, and if it is a corporate event any issues regarding corporate identity which are pertinent to the exhibition such as the company colours. If your company will be responsible for producing any banners or posters for the exhibitors' stands, you will need to inform the exhibitors

A Punch and Judy show.

of the deadline for receipt of their 'copy' (ie the wording that should be displayed on the items).

The administration process will be very similar to that for an event, namely:

- Contact reports.
- Flow charts.
- Contracts and payments not only to suppliers but by exhibitors for their stand.
- A technical rider to adhere to on both sides.
- Budgets.

You may also wish to prepare other documents such as:

- Schedules.

- Names of staff who are to man the stand.
- Any unusual requirements, such as a water supply to a particular stand.

Unlike a show or presentation scenario where people only see one side of the event, if your stand is open on three sides or the audience can access all sides, the finish is crucial. Cables, lights, and any other 'feed' to the stand has to be co-ordinated with the stand, meet health and safety requirements and be finished to a very high standard. In other words, it should be possible to walk around the stand without seeing gaffer tape, bags, plugs and sockets, cables or anything else that would ruin the finish or from the health and safety viewpoint be a trip hazard or present some other danger.

3   PRE-PRODUCTION

Pre-production is probably the most intense period of preparation for your event. You have been involved in regular monthly meetings with your client and your planning and internal meetings should be running smoothly.

After all the days or even months of planning, it all seems to come together at once. There will usually be new people to brief, such as show callers, stage management, the now expanded logistics and production teams, crew, drivers and many more. Even if you are working by yourself you will still need to formalize the 'mechanics' of the event. There will be a lot of information to distribute to a wide range of people. As team leader, event producer or project manager, most of this information will have originated from you or from the meetings that you have attended.

You will also have been keeping a close watch on all the various items or sections that require your client's approval, whether they

> 'Far too many clients ignore the obvious golden rules – unless you are Laurence Olivier, the audience will be ready to move on after 20 minutes, so keep the presentation short and stick to one objective and no more than a couple of key messages. Unfortunately office politics and fear of the senior executives involved usually gets the better of common sense.'
>
> *Simon Hambley, Acclaim!*

are directly your responsibility or the responsibility of other members of your team. This is the time to do a final check and assess what issues remain outstanding. In many cases the last items to be finalized are videos and scripts, which are often worked on until the famous eleventh hour.

If you are in any doubt, a final meeting with your client contact may be of help to clarify any areas which need attention.

NOTES FOR SPEAKERS

You will find it useful to provide the client and any speakers with a document summarizing all relevant information. You may have specific instructions and information about your rehearsal schedule, the stage itself or other points specific about your event. You must not assume that your client contact has passed on every detail to the 'cast' (in other words, your speakers). In addition, do not assume that any of your speakers have taken part in a similar event previously. This event may be the first time they have spoken on stage on behalf of this company, or this could even be their first time ever on stage.

You may have been involved with rehearsals of any speeches, which will be useful as it will give you an insight into the personalities of the individuals involved and a guide to what they are planning to say and what support they will need in terms of images, charts or words.

Your notes for speakers may include the following:

- Information about the venue (this may include parking, accommodation and other instructions.
- A short 'who's who': a guide to who the people are on site.
- The speaker's own schedule: when they should be on site, and what they should expect, for example a tour of the set, a description of the lectern or podium, a rehearsal with auto-Q and when the main run-through for the event will be held.
- If appropriate, mention the dress code for speakers for this event.
- A running order showing the order in which the speakers appear and estimated running times.

If inexperienced speakers have been working on their own presentations, it may be appropriate to remind them of some basic presentation guidelines.

- More than four bullet points per 'slide' will be difficult to read.
- If there is an event 'background', remind speakers that it should be used.
- Advise against the use of complicated graphs that are only referred to fleetingly. Unless the speaker is distributing a handout to the audience, the audience will not

'Maintaining and nurturing relationships with your suppliers will be one of the most important jobs for you as a logistics manager as you frequently have to turn to them for last-minute help and assistance. Knowing your suppliers and being able to put a face to a name whilst asking for the impossible will see you through many difficult situations.'

Emma Chesters,
Freelance Logistics Manager, UK

have time to 'read' the slide and their point will be lost.
- It may be useful to sum up at the end, with a slide that says 'If there is one thing that I want you to remember from this presentation it is ...' This will help to focus the audience back onto the message.

It will be important to ensure that you also go through a similar communication process with your suppliers and crew.

TECHNICAL OR PRODUCTION ELEMENTS

You (or your technical or production manager) will have contracted all the suppliers needed to supply items such as lighting, sound, scenic transport, projection equipment and auto-Q.

Some of these suppliers may well have attended no more than one briefing meeting held several months earlier. It may be helpful to call them in to 'walk them through' the event so that they are aware of all the elements of this particular event. For example, whilst their responsibilities may begin and end in the main presentation area, a supplier may need to know what will be happening in other areas which could affect their work, for example whether access will be required to other rooms, or the usual challenge of loading out the main room ready for a gala dinner or to make way for the next company who is to use the space. This meeting (the 'pre-production briefing') will also allow you to introduce all the suppliers to one another.

Whilst suppliers usually issue their crew or staff with their own schedules, it is usual for the producer or technical manager to draw-up a 'crew bible'. This will include basic information on the event title, the client's name and the objective of the event. It may also include the following:

- Crew contact list, including phone numbers, company names and heads of departments.
- Crew hotels: check in and check-out times maps, phone numbers and who is in which hotel, transfer arrangements between the hotel and the venue information, and perhaps site plans of the various rooms that you will be using. If the client will be using the same hotel, it is probably worth reminding the crew of this.
- On site catering arrangements.
- Car parking arrangements.
- Any financial instructions such as reimbursement for travel expenses.
- On site dress code: will you be providing a 'uniform' with the company logo (often known as 'swag'). If not, what should they wear – should members of the crew who will be visible to those attending the event wear suits?
- Security passes or 'laminates' and any restricted areas on site, if applicable.
- Your company's health and safety or behaviour policy with respect to accidents, lost property, alcohol on site, illegal substances, and your policy on unacceptable behaviour.
- The on-site schedule for the whole event.
- For outdoor events, consider including a copy of the script for the show for staff on the outskirts of the event so that they will know what is happening even if they are removed from the main action.
- If the event is to take place overseas, information on currency, vaccinations, travel arrangements and any other issues.
- Consider also providing a smaller A5 version of the crew bible for your own team.

Do not assume that all members of your crew will know all the other crew members, where they can collect 'comms' (radios), where the crew room is, or who is the on-site producer. A well informed crew will have more confidence,

'They (logistics) frequently are thought of as the bottom of the pile of the event team! We are known, amongst other things, as the tea, biscuits and transportation people. In some ways, it's a fair summary, but most clients, event organizers and production companies do actually realize that it is generally the logistics of an event which makes or breaks it. However good the creative ideas, however many fabulous speakers there are, if the logistics aren't fabulous, then this is what delegates remember.'

Emma Chesters,
Freelance Logistics Manager, UK

a better understanding of the aim of the event, and will be able to respond more efficiently to any emergencies.

Of course the larger and more complicated the event, the more sections there will be to your crew bible. It may be helpful to also provide a copy of the guide (or of relevant sections) to the venue and your main point of contact with your client.

Touring Overseas

Whilst many people are seasoned travellers, if they are to travel as an organized group, they will need comprehensive instructions. For some reason, in this situation even the most dynamic of people stop thinking and wait for orders.

Advice on currency and exchange rates may be useful, along with advice on any inoculations or immunization necessary and general information such as 'don't drink the water'. Any visa requirements should, hopefully, have been dealt with well in advance. You may also wish to provide any important cultural information about the country in which you will be working, such as codes of conduct, dress codes, and religious festivals.

On tour.

You may consider asking the crew to alert you to any medical conditions or any medication that they are taking in case of a medical emergency. You may also wish to keep a record of the crew's issue dates and number of passports in case they are lost or stolen. While overseas you may find yourself in the unusual position of being a confidante for lonely people, or visiting police stations in the middle of the night to 'rescue' members of your team or crew.

ENTERTAINERS AND GUEST SPEAKERS

Your event may include guest or celebrity speakers who will need their own set of instructions and information. Their agent or manager will probably provide a list of requirements not dissimilar to the 'rider' for a band.

The rider or contractual requirements usually centre on issues relating accommodation, travel, food and rehearsal time or sound checks. This should be reviewed carefully to assess any cost implications for your budget. If at all possible, try to obtain a telephone number or other method of contacting your guest speaker directly nearer show time, in case a situation arises where you are unable to speak to their agent or manager.

Guest speakers or celebrities appearing in the main event will rely on you for basic information about dress code, timings and some background to the event so that they can tailor their presentation or role to the event. At rehearsals you should be prepared to ease

'The more famous a person is, the more people will stand back or be embarrassed or too shy to approach; it is up to you to make the first move. Your "star" will thank you for being friendly and professional and will know that they can come back to you if they have any questions.'

Andrew Killian,
Freelance Stage Manager, UK

them into the show, introducing them to the main players and generally making them feel welcome.

It may be wise to allocate a member of your team to look after your star entertainer for the duration of the event. When the event is running, it will be difficult for you to abandon what you are doing in order to deal with whatever crisis is happening, imaginary or otherwise. It may pay dividends in the long term to have someone who can be at the star's beck and call without causing disruption to the main event or other items on the schedule.

If you are using a band at your event, either as a stand alone part of the entertainment or for the dance or cabaret, you will have to ensure that they have time to set up their instruments, fold-back (the speakers which enable the musicians to hear themselves play) and for a sound check.

This is notoriously difficult to do if the room that they will be performing in is adjacent to the room where the main event is being held. It is unlikely that you will be working in a totally sound proof environment and you will need to be aware of this when scheduling set up and

Claudio Abbado with the then European Community Youth Orchestra, Bratislava 1987.

sound check times. If the band is to play in the room where dinner will be served, it is inevitable that the performers will want to sound check when the room is being prepared by the event catering staff, and noise and light will be an issue on both sides.

Orchestras, big bands or smaller classical ensembles also require set up time. Their stage manager will need to lay out the stand and chairs in their usual performance formation, but instead of a sound check, an orchestra will want a 'seating rehearsal'. This is exactly what it sounds like, they check that they have enough room to play their instruments and crucially, that they can see to play, in other words, they need to check that they can clearly read the music on their music stand. You will need to have the lighting crew standing by with the correct lighting state 'up' and be ready to make adjustments for anyone who finds that they are blinded by a lantern or sitting in the dark.

Singers or solo performers will of course have their own 'riders' and will often require access to the stage in order to get the feel of the room. Of course if they are performing with musicians, they will be part of the sound check.

Of course, you should remember that you may need to provide food and drink for the performers. You may need to allocate a suitable waiting room or area in addition to the dressing or changing room.

Remember that although the discussion above centres on the event itself and arrangements for when you are on site, all this must be factored into schedules and budgets.

THE SCRIPT AND THE RUNNING ORDER

Even if you have not been involved in the creation of the speakers' presentations, you will be given a vital piece of information: the script. The script should ideally contain details of everything that happens from the moment that the audience arrive and you start the show through to the end, including:

- Who is speaking when and for how long.
- Whether they have a 'name slide' (a 'slide' showing their name and title).
- Whether videos will be shown, and how these fit into the schedule.
- Coffee breaks.
- Lunch breaks.
- Any question and answer sessions, or discussions on stage or from the audience.
- Any awards and presentations.
- Any reveals, for example of an new product, including details of any stage effects such as smoke or pyrotechnical effects.

You may also wish to note any requirements for changes in lighting (for example dimming lights when the show starts or when videos are playing on a screen). The example of a running order shown below could be expanded to form the basis for your script.

Whilst you are pulling this script together, you will inevitably reveal some gaps in your knowledge. Some of these queries can only be answered on site, for example where speakers will be sitting prior to their entrance, exits and other similar concerns. You may have already had conversations with the client about any music that may be played for the audience 'walk-in', and it may be that something has been commissioned and composed especially for the event. Try to note as much detail as possible in your script to make sure that nothing is overlooked.

The only difference between a script and a running order is the content. The running order is just a list of major actions. Even if you are responsible for a gala dinner you will still have a running order of what will happen at what time.

Star Events Ltd

Event: **Date:**

Running Order	Speakers	Duration	Other
10.00	Delegates registration, coffee		
10.20	Delegates into room		
10.30	Event Starts		
10.31	Opening Video	2.30	
10.33	MD opening speech, welcome and overview	25 mins	Radio mic
10.53	VT2. Sales overview	2.50	
10.55	Hand over to Sales Director	30 mins	From lectern
11.25	Hand over to Finance Director	25 mins	Lectern
11.50	Coffee etc		
12.10	Audit	30	
12.40	VT3		
	Lunch		

Document issue date:

Sample running order.

The start of the load in after a marquee has been built.

You will need quite a few copies of the running order as most of the crew (for example, lighting, sound, auto-Q, and 'speaker support' operators, cameras, video, logistics) will require a copy. The show caller will need a full script and will work in close contact with auto-Q to track any script changes that speakers may make during rehearsals.

YOUR OWN INFORMATION PACK AND EQUIPMENT

As project manager for the show, you will need to ensure that you have sufficient information with you when you travel to the show, for example your copy of the script and running order (along with some spare copies just in case). It will also be important to have to hand the file containing the contracts with the suppliers and any insurance documents. This may be vital if any last minute queries or disputes arise with suppliers during the event.

If your company has been responsible for creating videos or information packs for delegates, you will need to ensure that these are also delivered safely to the event. If at all possible, double check that the information packs are compiled correctly and ensure that any videos are clearly labelled. Remember to take spare copies in case of emergencies

Other items may include the following.

• On site kit box or production box. Sometimes this is called a 'project co-ordinators kit'. This is a miniature version of your office with your company letterhead, comp slips, and assorted stationery to help you function away from home. It may also contain personal items such as a small repair or sewing kit; a small shoe cleaning kit; a dry cleaning pad for de-spotting suits; and face powder (for shiny faces and bald heads).

- You may want to include chocolate, snacks and other treats to keep you all going during hectic periods.
- A selection of classical and 'pop' CDs or tapes, in case you need additional music during the event.
- Electrical or marking tape for marking the position of furniture and so on.
- Accident report book or forms.
- Copies of all suppliers' risk assessments.
- Show videos.
- Any awards or prizes for which you are responsible.

- Any spare plans or designs that may be needed as reference.
- All your show files for this event.
- Some ready made 'Reserved' signs for speakers' seats, VIP tables, and so on.
- Post cards for dressing rooms, showing the names of occupants.
- Coloured marking tape for marking position of furniture on stage.
- Stopwatch.
- A small emergency cleaning kit with cloths, cleaning spray and washing up liquid.

The contents of this box will evolve with you over the years until you have it just as you want it.

With the final client meeting over and all your crew bibles posted, the office packed up and ready to go, it is time to go on site.

4 SHOW TIME

The show is now just a few days away and you are on site. You may arrive a few days in advance of the actual show, although this is not always the case. You might be working on a road show in which case the load in (when the set and all the technical elements are physically loaded in to the building) and the build (the construction of the set, lights and so on) may happen just a few hours before the show or event.

On a road show you may have allowed for double crews in order that they can 'leapfrog' one another, with crews working on alternate venues so that the next venue can be prepared while the show takes place in the previous venue. However, budget limitations normally preclude this.

If you are working on an outdoor event or a special sporting or unusual event, you may have been on site weeks or months prior to the event rehearsing volunteer performers. There will still come a time when the set or site dressing has to be finished prior to the event proper and the site is open to the public or audience.

Dresses waiting to be claimed. ECYO (now the EUYO) Granada, Spain.

Whatever type of event you are working on, you will be undertaking very similar processes leading up to a point when the delegates or paying audience walk into the venue. The areas that you will need to know are being addressed and completed are discussed in the next section. You will see that one of the key pieces of advice will be 'never assume'.

BEFORE THE SHOW

If this is your first time on site and you are arriving when the load in has commenced, it can be disconcerting to see a mass of people busy working. The discussion below covers the areas to be completed prior to the first client or performer arriving on site, and assumes that the stage and technical areas are under the control of your production manager or technical manager. However, you will be in close contact with these members of your team for the duration of the build or set-up. Even if you are not directly responsible for any of the following areas, you will still need to check everything is in hand.

The Backstage Area

Whilst this is usually the domain of your technical team, representatives of your client may wish to come backstage before the event. They may need to look at the auto-Q and the speaker support, or possibly just wish to satisfy their curiosity as to the set up behind the scenes.

Whilst you will be used to the gloomy nature of the backstage area, your clients or speakers may not be and any potential hazards must be clearly marked with white or other tape. One of your responsibilities will be to make sure that all your speakers have been familiarized with the whole area when they arrive, in order to give them a feel for the environment that they will experience when the lights are in show conditions.

Dressing or Changing Rooms

You should always check the dressing rooms. You may need to arrange extra furniture or you may need to provide a special environment for performers who have made specific requests. Unfortunately you may find it necessary to make sure that they are clean, as they may well have not been cleaned since the last event. Including a small cleaning kit in your on-site box will be essential. Regardless of your job title, there may come a time when you will find yourself cleaning toilets or washroom facilities.

The rooms that you are using should have name cards on them and for larger events a list should be displayed to help people find their rooms. Even at small events you may want to clearly mark any rooms that will be used by your client in order to prevent anyone else inadvertently using them.

If children are to be involved on your event, you will need to observe any relevant local guidelines or laws. Most will be commonsense: children should have separate dressing rooms from adults and there must be toilets or showers for their sole use only and clearly marked.

If you are working with a logistics manager or team you will have been working together regarding catering and refreshment requirements for your clients and performers. Otherwise, it will be down to you to liaise with the management of the venue to ensure that all the rooms are suitably equipped and that items are replenished as appropriate.

Event Office

At larger events it may be appropriate to set up an event office, and this will become the hub of the event. It will have a high level of traffic and it will be the main information point prior to the event (while registration tables or front desks are not staffed). However you chose to design the layout of the event office you will

46

need to make sure that there is room for people to work, with space for computers, telephones and general workspace, along with a meeting area. If accommodation is tight, all this may need to take place within one room.

Catering

If you are feeding your crew on your event, an area for this should be allocated either by you, your logistics manager or the venue. This needs to be clearly marked and if there are any changes you should communicate this to all your team. You will not have a happy crew if they have to walk all over the building trying to find where their meal will be served.

Stage

The stage is the most important area for the event. Whilst it usually comes under the control of your production or technical manager, they will have other issues to distract them, and you should remain aware of this area. The figure shows how the team works on the technical side.

As the time when the speakers will arrive for their first rehearsal approaches, you will need to keep a close watch on the actual state of the stage platform and its environs. As the focus of all the work, tool kits, ladders and spare equipment will gradually accumulate on and

around it, and it is quite normal for the clearing up process to happen at the last moment. You may need to request cleaners from the venue for dusting or vacuuming and you may need to call in the crew to move their equipment and help with the general tidy up, whilst your production manager carries on organizing the technical side ready for the first rehearsal. Check that all cables running across the floor are either covered or taped down to avoid tripping hazards.

If the client's logo is being used on the lectern or on the scenery, mark this as a priority on your checklist, as you do not want the client to notice a mistake before the event has even started.

BASIC SHOW PREPARATION

Whilst you have been busy away from the stage, hopefully your show caller and lighting designer have decided on some basic show states, such as the video state, lectern state, walk-up state and the audience walk-in. Of course this may have been covered in numerous design or special effects style meetings, but it easy to forget the most basic sequences, such as dimming the house lights when the show starts. Never assume that the show caller and the lighting designer are going to do this in

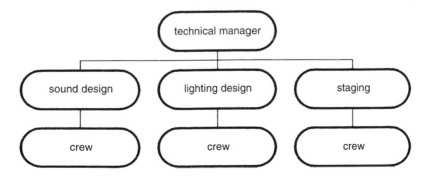

Organization chart for technical team on site.

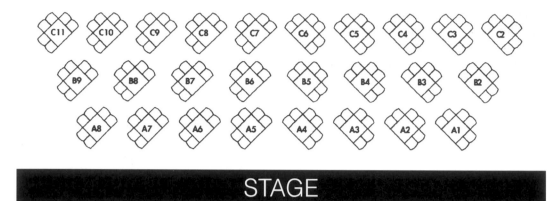

STAGE

Plan showing layout for a cabaret style seating arrangement.

your absence; always check that the basic decisions have been made. If you have asked your logistics team to organize water for the lectern or for the speakers, check that this has been done and that it will arrive in the correct form, for example in bottles or in plastic glasses.

You should check that your show caller has been through all the show videos with the operator backstage and that the videos have been arranged in the correct sequence. If you have 'sim-tran' (simultaneous translators) on site and there is time, take this opportunity to show them videos to help them prepare to translate any voiceover. If certain videos have been dubbed for different audiences, make sure that these are clearly labelled for your operator.

If the simultaneous translators will sit in booths at the back of the auditorium, check that these areas have all the necessary equipment. You will also need to set out headsets or ear pieces on the delegates' chairs each day, and check that they work.

Make sure that you locate a suitable spot where you can sit and watch the rehearsals, with easy access to the stage and speakers. Remember to ensure that you can communicate with your show caller.

Auditorium

You will have discussed how you wish the audience seating to be laid out, possibly including tables. If this is being done on the show day only and not for rehearsals, then obviously you will need to arrange seating for your client and the speakers. The figure shows the audience seating set out in a cabaret style.

Exhibition Area and Break-out Rooms

Whilst you are focussed on the main presentation area, there may also be much work to be done on other areas that are also part of your event.

If there is an exhibition area, your production manager's time will always be split between the two areas. Along with break-out rooms for smaller sessions, exhibitions are often left until the last minute. If the planning for the main presentation falls behind schedule or if the technical or build staff are unexpectedly called away, there is a danger that exhibitions may place enormous stress on the team

Delegate Registration Area

This is usually the domain of your logistics staff. They will have arranged all the badges, systems, signs, staff and furniture to make this a friendly, smooth and efficient process.

If the delegates are staying in the hotel where the event is to be held, it may be helpful to arrange for a separate check in system set apart from normal hotel guests. Members of the logistics team should be on hand to assist with questions and enquiries. You should be aware that checking into the hotel is a very important part of your event. Your logistics team must smooth over delicate situations and reassure late arrivals, and deal with lost luggage and a host of other problems before your audience ever comes near the presentation room. Members of the team may have to work outside in all weathers overseeing coaches, cars and parking. They, like all your team, will respond well to regular checks that they are surviving whatever has come their way.

REHEARSALS

Make sure that your crew has an early call to allow them to complete any checks or work prior to your client arriving on site, and mark it clearly as 'crew call' on any schedules or notices.

If your logistics team are in regular contact with your speakers, ask them to check anticipated arrival times and if possible to remind the speakers of the time that they are expected to arrive for rehearsals. Consider doing a room-drop of instructions, ready for their arrival at the hotel.

Remember that your motto for all of this time should be 'never assume'. Even though you have sent out comprehensive speakers' notes and talked your client through them, the worst mistake you could make is believing that all of your speakers are experienced enough to know what your expectations will be of them for these rehearsals. While most speakers will turn up fully prepared, inevitably there will be one or two who will arrive with no speech formalized, and you will have to cope with this situation as best you can.

Luckily, there are several tactics that you can use to move people around and accommodate all the various levels of expertise.

• If the speaker will have some sort of visual aid to support the presentation, the speaker will need to go through this with the operator, or check that their laptop (or whatever equipment they have brought with them) is

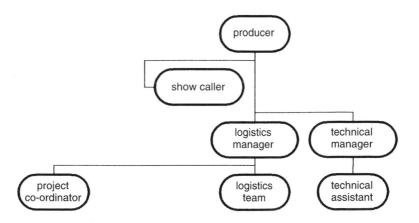

Organization chart on site showing show caller and producer positions.

compatible with the equipment available at the venue.

- If you are using an auto-Q, the speaker may have to spend time with the auto-Q operator to go through any changes they have made to their presentation. For a novice speaker, this may be a very good private rehearsal opportunity. Most auto-Q operators are used to hand-holding nervous or inexperienced clients and can help them to rehearse quietly out of sight of their peers. A stage manager can help by guiding speakers around the backstage sections whilst you deal with speakers on stage.

- You will need each speaker to check out the stage, where everything is, how they enter and exit and where from and to. They will have to get a feel for whatever lighting states you are using, and you might want to discover whether they would be happier if they could see the audience or whether they prefer a black 'hole' in front of them. A sound check is crucial too, to check that their particular timbre is catered for and also as an introduction to the sound operator who may be fitting them with a radio microphone. You should also make sure that they are aware of where they will need to go in order to be fitted with their microphone prior to the actual event, and that they know where to return the microphone at the end of the show.

During these rehearsals, check with your show caller that the scripts being used are up-to-date and that any changes are making their way to sim-tran, if appropriate. They will need to know about all and every change, from words to running order, including any cuts.

Check with your client if there is an order of priority for your speakers and if necessary ask them to point VIPs out to you.

You may have cameras at your event, perhaps so that an image of the speaker can be shown on a screen behind them. However, if any speakers are suffering from hair loss, a shiny head will upstage their performance. You may want to have a word with them privately, and suggest the use of anti-shine powder (which you should have handy in your on-site kit).

The 'Stagger Through' Rehearsal

Once all your speakers are ready and have been through all the various processes with scripts, auto-Q, sound check and lighting check, you will need to carry out a 'stagger through' (or 'Q-Q rehearsal). For this rehearsal, you will not be expecting your speakers to read or perform the whole of their presentation. The speakers will need to take guidance from you as to where in the script you require them to start or finish if the script leads into video or specific actions on the stage, car reveals or similar.

As in any rehearsal, speakers can feel quite isolated standing alone on the stage when it appears that everything has stopped and no-one is telling them what is happening. You may be reviewing videos, or making other changes that the presenters are unaware of, and it is essential that you keep them informed as to what is going on and explain how long it is going to take before the rehearsal continues. Whilst you and your team will be on head-sets, or can communicate with one another in some other way, your speakers may have no idea what is going on. It can be quite demoralizing to be staring out into darkness and hearing the occasional murmur of voices and laughter, and it is important to reassure them periodically.

Technical Rehearsals

Technical rehearsals usually happen prior to the arrival of the speakers, if sufficient time is available. It gives your team an opportunity to see what the show will actually involve.

However, if there have been any technical problems or perhaps if your speakers are heavily involved in certain aspects of the show, you may find yourself rehearsing the technical elements of the show for the first time during the 'stagger through'. Again, you will need to ensure that the communication process is working well during these rehearsals.

The Run Through

If you have been fortunate enough to have had technical rehearsals and a 'stagger through', any teething problems should have been ironed out and the run through should be straight forward.

Your main objective during these rehearsals is to establish the exact running time of each section of your event. There can be some unpleasant surprises at this point if you have not had time to rehearse and check the speakers' presentations. It may be that your speaker is expecting to be able to repeat a presentation given in the past, even though it is far longer than required or expected.

Your client may be able to help with any mediation between yourself and the speaker when cuts are suggested, but if it is too late to make any changes the ramifications are often fairly dramatic. If schedule changes are needed, you should involve all your various heads of departments. Make a list of the things that you are aware that it will affect and be prepared for all your team to add to this. Here is an example of what could be affected by an over-long presentation.

> 'The company must ensure there is a sizable contingency fund. However well planned there are always contingencies.'
> *Bill Vestey, Director of Public Affairs,*
> *Sony UK Ltd.*

- Catering may be affected as the timing for coffee breaks and meal breaks may be altered.
- Travel arrangements could be affected. Delegates may be on a tight schedule for flights to take them onto their next appointment.
- There may be technical issues. If your load out or get out is delayed, will it have an impact on transport, the venue or your next venue?

It is usually the logistics department which will take the brunt of all these changes, and assist by taking on any negotiations and changes whilst you carry on with organizing the event as a whole.

Band Sound Checks

If you are fortunate enough to have a stage manager or similar on board specifically to look after the entertainment, all you will need to do is to be aware that this is happening. If you are in charge of the entertainment as well as the main event, hopefully you will have organized the schedule so that you can check on the venue where the entertainment will be provided. A sound operator will be needed for the rehearsal and also, if possible, the correct lighting state should be used so that they get a feel for the performing environment.

Depending on your schedule and how long the entertainers have between the sound check and their part of the show, you will need to make sure that they know where their dressing rooms are, where they are being fed, and so on.

Health and Safety

On site, in most situations checking that your working environment is safe will be largely a matter of common sense. Your production manager will often have checked many issues

A band playing at an outdoor event.

before you even arrive on site. You should be alert to the last few details, such as cables that could trip people up, obstacles that you could walk into or that might cause an obstruction in case of an emergency, steps that may need lighting or white tape markings on the floor to help guide delegates.

Requirements governing hours of work, meal breaks and working conditions will vary depending on where you are in the world. Again the basis for all of this is common sense. An overtired and hungry crew will be an inefficient and potentially dangerous crew.

Whilst this is obvious, it can be a difficult situation to balance against the expectations of your client. If you have to ensure that everything is ready for a rehearsal at 6.30am, your crew will have to be ready at least an hour

prior to this. If your client was late arriving or your rehearsal overran the night before, you might have the beginnings of a difficult day ahead for the whole team.

Some event companies charge overtime to their client if a pre-planned day goes over, for example, 14 hours. This can act as a deterrent for long meals and late arrivals, but does not prevent team members from working long hours. In the EU at the present time there are limits on the number of hours that an individual can work per week. After this limit has been reached, the individual must take time off. Even if your crew or team have signed waivers to avoid missing the show day, crucial rehearsal or whatever, you may still be working with crews who will insist on their right to time off.

Snagging

After the last rehearsal, you will need to tour the whole venue with your production manager and heads of departments to compile what is known as a 'snagging' list. This is the final list of things that may need attention before the show. Even if your site was immaculate prior to the rehearsals, anything from lighting to the seating or script changes may need further work prior to the arrival of the audience.

The End of the Day

Despite the fact that everyone may be tired or busy, you will need to get everyone together to sit and go through any issues that have arisen and ensure that everyone knows the time limit on any changes required.

When you set the crew call or time on site for the show day, be careful to emphasize when the crew are expected to be ready and on stand by. Be careful to always allow time prior to the stand by to make sure that everyone is ready.

Before the people representing your client leave for the night, check that they know the dress code for the show day and that they know what time you are expecting them.

THE STAGE MANAGER

Stage managers are more usually found in the theatre, but their experience may prove invaluable when staging an event.

Unlike a theatre play or show where the stage manager will have been involved with rehearsals for several weeks beforehand, the stage manager will have very little prior knowledge of the event. A pre-site meeting with the producer and other members of the team will give an idea of the design, running order and content of the show and where the stage manager will fit into the overall picture.

During the rehearsals, the stage manager may help to look after the speakers. It may be necessary to locate the speakers from the audience, guide them backstage, and make sure that they have radio microphones fitted.

Experience gained in the theatre will be a great asset in alerting the stage manager to what will be needed, everything from checking that steps or treads are clearly marked with white tape, to ensuring that there are clear routes and passageways backstage. The usual theatre 'tool-kit', such as torch, marking tape, clip board, and notepad will prove useful.

The timings of the event will not be the responsibility of the stage manager. Even if working on the cabaret or entertainment, the stage manager will be reacting to the client's schedule or priorities and taking instructions from the producer or show caller.

At an outdoor event the stage manager will probably be responsible for some performers' rehearsals, running orders, people movement and so on. Remember that on a large show the stage manager may well be based 30 minutes away from the 'mission control', and will need to make sure that everything needed is to hand.

THE SHOW CALLER

The show caller has a great deal of responsibility, acting as a source of information regarding scripts, corrections to running orders and general information to the crew. If there is no stage manager on the event the show caller may be the main point of contact for all the crew and as such will be crucial to morale.

As in a stage production, the success of the event will hinge on clarity of communication and accuracy of cues. The show caller should always be aware of the desired running time, being alert to sections running over or being shorter than planned, and will be responsible for passing this information to the producer.

It will be the show callers responsibility to seek out scripts, videos and any other elements needed to create the show or cuing script. Shortly after your arrival on site, a break will be required to allow the show caller to create the show script, and this will have been factored into the schedule prior to the first rehearsal.

If there are any technical problems during rehearsals or run throughs, the show caller will be expected to provide accurate commentary on what is happening. In an outdoor event, the show caller will probably have been involved for much of the rehearsals.

It is vital that the show caller is aware who will give clearance to start the event, as there can be a selection of people (logistics, client and producer) all trying to attract attention. A pair of binoculars can prove extremely useful if the show caller is to be seated at the back of the auditorium or high on a scaffold tower.

The role of the show caller will be very similar whether the event is to be held indoors or outdoors, although on a major ceremony there may be unusual things to cue, ranging from aeroplanes to battalions of soldiers or national flags being raised or lowered.

The Show

After all your hard work, the crucial moment has arrived and you are ready to let the audience in. Before they arrive, do the following:

- Check the lectern or podium to make sure that water, glasses and anything else specifically required for your show are in place.
- Check that 'reserved' signs are in place on the chairs for the speakers.
- Check with your production manager that the snagging list is done.
- Follow the old theatrical maxim and 'look up'. You will be amazed at the things that may have been missed, as people tend to look straight ahead of them.

- Use your own checklist of any specific points to note.
- Check that all the crew are in their required show 'uniform', if appropriate.
- Talk to all the crew to make sure that there are no unforeseen problems.
- Check that you know how to start the show. Do you know who will give you clearance to say that everyone has arrived and that you can start? Does your show caller know the process and sequence for this?
- Check that someone has been given the task of ensuring that all the speakers are ready.
- Is the stage ready, with the correct lighting and music playing for the start of the event?

Like all the actions that are part of staging an event, all the entries on the list above are obvious and logical but incredibly easy to forget when under stress. With the show safely started and running smoothly your own show list will tell you what you need to be doing next, from sound checks for bands to ensuring that break-out rooms are ready.

Whilst all is calm there are still things that could happen that you should be aware of: for example, the client might ask for additional guests to be catered for, flowers to be available as prizes, or a supply of extra champagne. This is where your PCN (product change notice) will be vital, as something ordered or requested under these circumstances is easily forgotten.

The Load Out

Whilst your logistic team are sending the delegates safely on their way, the crew will be dismantling all the technical elements of the show. If you are working on a road show, you may be working to a strict time limit and you may need to leave the venue before the load out has even started.

The stage suddenly becomes crowded with people. Jeremy Irons surrounded by crew, cameras and staff (Rio de Janeiro).

You and your production or technical manager will need to ensure that the venue is left as tidy as possible, and check with the venue management to establish if there are any outstanding problems or accounts remaining unpaid. Your event office and your production box will have been packed up at some point during the show day ready for it to be returned home or forwarded to the next venue.

Before leaving you need to check that you, or one of your team, have carried out the following:

- Collect up all video tapes, DVDs, CDs and any other show material that was handed out to the various departments for the show.
- If the show content was of a sensitive nature, you might be required by your client to return all scripts, running orders, auto-Q discs and scripts back to them, if not returned immediately after the show. (It has been known for a security guard to stand behind a show caller and, seconds before a presentation, hand the show

Audience in costume for a fête champêtre.

Goodwill

Before you leave the venue, remember to thank all your team – regardless of any glitches or mistakes, you may all be working together again in a few weeks' time and their goodwill may be vital. If any major mistakes have occurred (and this is an industry where you really are only as good as your last job), it is easy to make sure that anyone who has stood out as a problem is avoided in the future. But remember, this can also happen to you.

caller a script to follow which must be sight-read, guessing any video or other similar items and then whisk the script away the moment that the speaker has finished.)

• There may be a handful of lost property which must be returned to its owners. If you are lucky, you may be able to pass the lost property straight to your client, for the client to deal with.

With a successful event just completed it is time to relax. Hopefully your client has already thanked you and your team and everyone is happy.

5   THE DE-BRIEF

T he event has been a great success, and you are looking forward to meeting the client for a constructive de-brief, with hopefully some praise and a promise of another event. However, all the client wishes to say is that a bill has arrived that was never ordered. Of course, if you have been following all the procedures to the letter you will be able to produce a copy of the signed product change notice, but mistakes do happen.

This chapter will take you through the process of closing your 'event file' – the 'Reconciliation' (the term used for all the payments, reports, and meetings that take place in the weeks following an event, the thank you letters and the complaints).

PAYMENTS AND THE RECONCILIATION

Finance will always be at the forefront of everyone's minds. Even on a successful event you will be very conscious of your profit margins and what expenses may become a query for the client.

If your various processes of sign offs and product change notices have been successful then, other than human error, there should be no problems. Human error can include loss of any paperwork to selective amnesia regarding change requests. You should be able to back this all up with your own paper trail.

If you have an accounts department, there may be a meeting at some point to address any issues that the department may have. For example, a supplier may invoice for something that is not on the original purchase order, such as additional expenses, laundry or extra days worked. Resolving these issues can prove to be a lengthy process and you may be working to a deadline to close the event file to allow your accounts department to prepare the final invoice.

You will need to ensure that you sign off invoices from your team and any contractors promptly in order that they are paid as soon as possible. Remember that freelance staff may be reluctant to accept future work from companies which they perceive to be slow payers.

Some clients prefer to handle all payments to suppliers, as this allows them to see the actual spend and to forego paying any handling fee to the events company. In this situation, your meeting will be with the client's accounts department. You should go to this meeting with as much information on potential queries as possible.

'At the end of the day, however, there is nothing more satisfying than knowing you have been responsible for getting thousands of people from around the world to one place, on time and in one piece, and have fed, watered, housed and moved them around a strange city for a week without losing anyone. It's a hugely fulfilling experience!'

Emma Chester,
Freelance Logistics Manager, UK

You will need to draw up a spreadsheet that shows:

- What was the original budget figure.
- What was the actual spend, backed up with paperwork as necessary. Although you may not need to offer great detail regarding why a particular member of the crew has invoiced for a higher amount than originally anticipated, you should have a breakdown available (such as overtime or missed breaks) and an explanation of why it was necessary. If the extra expense cannot be resolved with the client, you should be prepared for it to be a hit against your profit margin.
- Either a balance that agrees or a deficit or other.

If you are providing your client with copies of product change notices, these should be attached to the spreadsheet in order to back up your figures. Whilst your client should have records of any budget sign-off discussions in its files, to save time you should make sure that you have copies of any relevant documents to hand at the meeting.

To make the process easier, prepare a mini document with a reference section, the original budget, and any other useful information, for example currency rates of exchange, any changes to the schedule, perhaps a summary of the history of the event and notes of any additional staff employed. Whilst it may appear that you are creating more paperwork, in the long run this should save time and help to ease the pressure at any finance meetings. If your finance meeting is held weeks after the event, the document you have prepared will serve as an *aide-memoire*. After all, you have created some good systems for the event, provided everyone with good clear concise information and as this is one of your final reports, you should maintain that same level of attention to detail.

If your schedule of payments has been for example 30% of the agreed fee on signing, or receipt of contract or purchase order, 30% at a midway point, 30% on the day of the event and 10% within a certain time after the event, then hopefully your final payment will cover the complete spend. Remember that the final payment, whatever proportion of the total fee it may be, may never be paid by the client if there is disagreement on the final spend.

CONCERNS AND LITIGATION

If your event has been a great success, be careful to thank all concerned. You may find that your client also wants to send thanks, which is always rewarding for a crew that have gone that extra mile for your event. However it may be that something relating to the event may lead to you or your company becoming involved in some form of legal action.

If you are a freelance event manager, you should carry third party liability insurance for yourself, but if there has been a serious incident, this will not cure the problem for you or your company. Luckily serious accidents or even fatalities are extremely rare, and whilst they are incredibly distressing, it is crucial to report such incidents as soon as possible, while the details are clear in your mind.

THE DE-BRIEF

The de-brief marks the end of your event. Even if it has been a great success and all the financial concerns have been dealt with, you will have to be prepared for some unexpected feedback.

Occasionally, complaints will be raised for the first time at a de-brief meeting. Frustratingly, it will often be an issue that could have been dealt with on site at the time of any 'incident', such as a slow moving car park, mobile toilets that were not satisfactory, a sign

The de-brief

'De-briefs can often be rather depressing when everyone concentrates on the things that either did not work or went wrong. However, often, the visitors are totally unaware of problems. Concentrate on the positives and remember the mistakes so that they are not repeated in the future.'

Bill Vestey,
Director of Public Affairs, Sony UK Ltd.

that had fallen down, or sound speakers that were too loud.

Of course, all feedback is useful and you can learn from the experience to prevent a similar problem arising at the next event but it can leave you feeling really quite deflated if an issue has seriously upset one of your clients.

It can be tempting to get into a heated discussion about any problems, especially if members of your team feel that they personally are being criticized. If you are not able to shift the focus or contribute to the discussion positively, then it may be preferable to suggest that the discussion is continued 'off-line' (that is outside the meeting), rather than cause any embarrassment to any of the parties involved. Also, by doing this, you may be able to privately dissuade any of your team from any further discussion. This is obvious, basic advice but in an important meeting stress can affect people in different ways, even more so when they feel that their reputation is at risk.

If your client has agreed to complete a feedback questionnaire about the event, this will give you the real feeling for the event, along with any feedback from the delegates. Remember to pass on all feedback to your team and to any suppliers.

At the feedback meeting you may also be able to glean information about any future events planned and make sure that your client is aware of your interest.

6 OUTDOOR EVENTS

Although much of the process involved in organizing an outdoor event will be the same as those for events held indoors, there will be some specific issues.

One of the deciding factors on your event, the response to the brief and all the decisions that you will be making with your team, will be the demographics of your audience. In other words, who they are and what their expectations will be. Consider the different types of audiences who may attend anything from the village fête to a rock concert, with all the variations between, such as classical open air concerts, weddings, and craft shows. Consider issues such as security, space per person, queues, available facilities, the behaviour of the crowd, and noise. This will help you to understand the choices that are made either by necessity or even by law.

Audience arriving with hampers and chairs for a fête champêtre.

THE VENUE

Your venue may be a field or green field site, or an athletics stadium. Outdoor sites come with their own unique qualities, but there is an unwritten law that the more beautiful a site is, the more problematical it can be. Before you or your client commit yourselves, take a step back and review all the following points.

Even if you are producing a small garden or village fete, you will have to address the problems of rubbish disposal, power supply, catering facilities, toilets, first aid and car parking, and of course a risk assessment must be carried out and any health and safety issues dealt with. For example, for a lavish wedding with a large marquee in a garden, you may have to consider the weather, the facilities available, the size of marquee and car parking for guests.

Some of the major issues to be considered are shown below.

- No power: you may need generators, but arranging them to be placed on site may prove to be difficult.
- No water: if water mains cannot be accessed, you may need to use water bowsers.
- No toilets: sourcing the right number of portable toilets for your event and placing them on your site may be a challenge.
- Consider the site capacity: how many people, audience and backstage can your particular choice of venue accommodate?
- Telephones, communication, or public address system: these may have to be provided and, of course, there will be a cost factor involved. The more beautiful the spot, the more likely it is that some of the cell or

Building a temporary bridge over a waterfall to allow 3,000 people to cross safely at night.

Wagons arriving on site.

mobile phones on site will have no network coverage. When you and your team members are visiting the site, it is useful for you all to check your mobile phones to see which service provides the best local coverage or signal.

• No dressing rooms or weather cover. Hiring marquees is an obvious solution.

• No rehearsal space of a similar size to the venue. If you cannot have access to the venue for the months, weeks or days prior to the event, you will need to find another space of a similar size that is available to you during that period.

• No access to the venue until the load in day.

• Lack of car parking. Bad weather on the day of the event can turn a field used as a temporary car park into a sea of mud. You may need to make an allowance in your budget for Trakway (a form of metal or plastic plating linked together that prevents vehicles from sinking into mud), but you will need permission before using equipment like this as it can damage the ground. If possible, arrange for use of a tractor in case of emergencies, as four-track vehicles may not be powerful enough to free cars that have become stuck. For an evening event, if your car park has no lighting you will have to budget for the cost of providing this.

• Lack of catering facilities. Catering trucks and wagons can be brought onto the site but you may encounter access problems. They will need power, waste disposal and access to water. Strict guidelines relate to catering on site and you should check for any local restrictions. Of course, in many cases your caterers will be able to advise you on the requirements in their local area.

- Lack of signage for pedestrians and vehicles. Many companies specialize in producing signs, so once you have decided on what is needed there should be little difficulty in arranging for suitable signs to be manufactured.
- Access problems. There may be difficulties with the access into your site, such as small country lanes, rough terrain which vehicles must cross, and issues regarding access for disabled members of the audience or staff. You may need to build physical crossing points or bridges, and most local authorities will have a specialist member of staff who will be able to advise you.
- Noise considerations. Within built up areas you may have to finish rehearsals or stop working at certain times. The event may

well be inspected and given a decibel limit for rehearsal and performance days.

- Lack of staff. Any event will require stewards, security, car park attendants and first aid staff. If the event is very remote, you may need to address the problem of transporting the staff to the site and arranging accommodation.
- Weather, good and bad, and windy. Rain, sun, thunder, lightning and strong winds can bring havoc to your event. Remember to check the prevailing winds for your site. Also, discover where the sun rises and sets and how this might affect your audience or performance, along with the times of sunrise and sunset. The weather may also restrict what you can or cannot build: marquees for example and any semi-permanent structures will all need special consideration.

Constructing a marquee.

MARQUEES

From fabulous creative designs which are attractive outside as well as inside through to functional 'tents' for events, marquees need to follow strict guidelines. They are also susceptible to wind, rain and extremes of weather. Some decisions may be made for you by budget restrictions, health and safety guidelines or the limitations of your site.

Your marquee supplier will advise you on:

- The size of marquee required for your audience (or the maximum number of people who may be accommodated inside a particular marquee).
- Flooring: options include soft coconut matting, hard flooring with carpet on top, or none at all.
- The number of doors or access and exit points required for the expected number of visitors.
- Emergency lighting, in case of a power cut.
- Generators for power supply for the marquee.
- Emergency exit signs for all exit points.
- Fire fighting and other emergency equipment.
- Dressing the interior of the marquee, in other words, whether to have a lining that covers poles, joins and seams (some very elaborate linings are available for weddings and parties).
- Whether they also supply items such as balloons, drapes, dance floors, small stages and basic light and sound kits.
- Furniture: the marquee supplier may recommend the ideal furniture layout taking into account the number of guests and the size of the marquee.

If the floor is to be carpeted, some form of weather cover will be required to protect it whilst the crew and staff are setting up the marquee ready for the event. You may also want to provide a pathway of matting or similar leading to the main entrance to act as a dirt trap before the guests enter the marquee for the event itself.

Remember that a large state-of-the-art marquee can take five or six days to build, before any finishes are put in. There is usually a very large crew for erecting the larger marquees. Catering and other requirements may need to be added to the budget.

Marquees can be very cold in bad weather and you may need to consider heating. Of course they can also be extremely warm and may also need fans for cooling.

INSURANCE

A figure should also be included in your budget for insurance cover. It is important to use a broker with experience of outdoor events. Many companies provide cover for weddings, carnivals and small outdoor shows. You will need to provide an overview of your event, including any pyrotechnics. Weather cover is expensive but you may want to consider such insurance to cover the cost of extra equipment, marquees, Trakway and so on.

YOUR BUDGET

All of the above will have a considerable impact on your budget and you will need to contact specialist suppliers for quotes and expertise.

You may also have to add charges for emergency services. For example, the police in your area may make a nominal charge for assisting the traffic flow for a medium-size event. Of course if you are working on an Olympic-size event this cost may be covered by others, but it will be considerable. You should also allow for paramedics and other emergency aid. If you are using a voluntary service, they

> 'During rehearsals and the event itself, make sure there is someone from the company available who can make instant decisions. Things happen – you need to be able to react quickly.'
>
> *Bill Vestey,*
> *Director of Public Affairs, Sony UK Ltd.*

may welcome a donation and possibly some complementary tickets to your event.

You may have to create a secure environment for the event with fencing or a boundary. You will also need to hold discussions with the fire service and paramedics to ensure that you have allowed access for emergency vehicles in your design or plan. Making local police aware from an early stage of your planned event will alert them to any potential traffic problems, and they may offer to provide help with the arrival of your audience or guests.

Site Layout and Health and Safety

Your site plans will gradually change and evolve as your initial concept is modified to cope with the restrictions that the site and the laws and guidelines place on your event. They have to be drawn up from the moment you start 'designing' or creating your event and will be a constant source of reference. From the master plan showing the entire site to the plans of the various areas, these will have to be meticulously kept up to date for approval and for any inspections.

Health and safety is an issue no matter where you are in the world, and, if you are in any doubt your local council or state will have a list of recommended experts who can assist. In the UK, a specialist organization, the National Outdoor Events Association (NOEA),

can provide a list of accredited suppliers and a useful handbook. If you have any basic queries, such as how many mobile toilets will be required, this handbook will tell you. It will also provide information such as the current guidelines and recommendations for vehicle access and placement of catering facilities in relation to waste disposal. Many of the items covered you may never need to know, but if there are any problems relating to your event, you need to be sure that you have done everything possible to follow the guidelines. There is also a government handbook usually referred to as the 'blue guide', containing guidelines for rock concerts and other similar events.

If your site includes a lake or open water, you should consider whether to ring fence, light, or patrol the area. It is easy to overlook this, especially if you are using a site where there have never been any problems before, or in the wedding reception or garden fete scenario where the site includes an ornamental pond. It is your responsibility to consider the problem and include it in your risk assessment making and changes that are necessary. This is crucial when small children may attend the event.

If your event will conclude with a fabulous fireworks display, or indeed if pyrotechnics are used at any point, your supplier should be accredited, experienced and be able to follow local guidelines.

You will need to ensure that you have copies of all your suppliers' insurance documents and their own risk assessments, covering how they plan to deliver machinery or equipment to the site safely. The suppliers may have to supply you with a risk assessment for building any stands or set on site.

You, in turn, may have to provide a complete risk assessment for the whole event. If this is outside the area of your expertise, there are specialists who can help. It is crucial to carry out this process, not only for the safety of

When riggers or scaffolders are working off the ground, weather warnings for high winds or lightning will be very important.

the event and your audience, but to also ensure that your insurance cover will be valid.

MEETINGS AND COMMUNICATIONS

On a large scale event, many meetings will be required, and you may have to meet senior people who have 'civic' responsibility, for example, emergency planners, security forces, armed forces and other government or state offices, such as anti-terrorist officers. Inevitably, you will also be working with partner agencies, broadcast partners and sponsors, all with their own agenda and expectations. Your report forms and action lists will become even more important on this type of event, as will maintaining a full and complete paper trail in case of any queries.

You may want to re-think roles and responsibilities for members of your team in order that they have ownership of some of these new areas, or even employ additional experienced staff. For a very large scale event, it is simply not possible for one person to attend every meeting and continue to 'build' the event. If you do find yourself at the top of the pyramid, it is vital to make sure that you have the support staff you need, not only for your sanity but again for the sake of a safe, successful event. Everyone's skills will be tested on an event with thousands of performers and high audience expectations.

SCHEDULES

For a concert or similar event, your schedule is fairly straightforward, but could be affected by any of the following. For a large sporting event with an opening or closing ceremony you will need to factor in some other considerations.

Weather and weather days
Wherever you are in the world, the weather can play out-of-season tricks on you. When it gets near to show day and you are rehearsing for the last time, make sure you have a 'spare' day or a plan to fit in your final rehearsal if you have been rained off unexpectedly. You will be able to get a long-range weather forecast wherever you are in the world, although four-day forecasts are usually more accurate. One of the production assistants working with the technical management of the event will usually be tasked as 'weather monitor'. Aside from the usual information about rain and temperature, they play a crucial role by giving warning of possible lightning storms and high winds, which is essential for riggers and other members of the team and performers, working not only at high level, but on exposed ground.

Daylight
This may sound obvious, but when you are rehearsing large numbers of performers, you may not have additional lighting or generators on site. Your day will be ruled by the hours of daylight. Any lighting that will be needed for the show itself will obviously be focussed and checked at night when it is dark. This will affect your budget and schedules. In the northern hemisphere, you can check on the daylight situation or dusk exactly six months ahead of your event, as sunrise or sunset will be the same. For example for an event in September, you should look at the conditions in March, weather permitting.

Local conditions
If you are rehearsing in a built up area, you may have to keep a close check on sound levels for rehearsals and for the show day. This will impact on your schedule. You may also have to enforce silent working if any department will be working during the night.

Wildlife
Deer, snakes, birds and many other animals, can be interesting and unwelcome additions to your event. Local advice will be needed, and of course be mindful of disturbing their habitat and any potential hazards for your staff and the audience.

Rehearsals on site
These may run for weeks prior to the event. For a large choreographed ceremony pitch markers will be needed. These are usually plastic circles with a letter and number, which indicate to the performers where they have to be at specific points. Usually placed at one metre intervals, they form a grid over the grassed area of your stadium, and can be fixed with long plastic golf tees. Unfortunately, to avoid damage to the grass they will need to be lifted and placed each day leading up to the show and this can

'Always create a detailed timeline with job descriptions, especially when working with volunteers. This helps make the process seem less overwhelming and give the volunteers specific duties that they can accomplish and check off.'

Kerry Peavey, Freelance Sports Events Organizer, Texas, USA

take several hours at the start and close of each day. The choreographer or director will let you know their expectations for rehearsals. You will probably need a small sound system that the stage management of assistant choreographers can operate, a viewing platform from which the choreographer can watch the performers, radio microphones for the choreographers and the stage management, and suitable weather cover for the sound equipment.

SECURITY

If you have a lot of people on site for rehearsals, then you will need to ensure they have access to mobile toilets, weather cover, refreshments and first aid. If children will be involved in the event, you must follow all the relevant restrictions, laws and guidelines regarding separate facilities such as toilets and changing rooms and arrangements for parents/chaperones. If you are working with children, it is vital to ensure that you have a children's co-ordinator or adviser who is aware of the current legislation with regards to child safety and care.

Police or other checks may be made on you and your team on large events, and you should consider warning all your suppliers about this. If you decide to send out a form to all the suppliers and members of your team, advise them to be open about anything that might potentially hinder their application, as in the long run it will save time and embarrassment for all concerned. This is crucially a child-protection and anti-terrorism measure, and should be taken very seriously. All forms should be headed 'Strictly Private and Confidential' and should be treated as such.

Additional Paperwork

If you have been involved in the process of getting support for the event with volunteer performers, or presenting to local schools, you will need a system of checking who has been at rehearsals and who is missing.

Outdoor Events Survival Kit

Stage managers and field workers/crew, performers, volunteers should have with them in a named rucksack:

Wet weather gear.
Cold weather clothing, in other words layers, jumper, T shirt to cope with any vagaries of the weather.
Change of shoes.
Sun hat.
Sun barrier cream, no-one should be allowed to work in any capacity without this.
Water or refreshments.
Food.
A book.
Spare battery for comms, radio phone etc (crew only).
Pens, paper, script.
Torch.
Small first aid kit.
Personal medication as required.

Remind all personnel that no valuables should be carried in the rucksack.

Signing-in sheets will be part of your life on site and you will find that the choreographer or director will work closely with you to identify anyone who is continuously absent. If the event is a complicated one, there will be a point at which it is no longer possible to 'slot someone back in' after a few missed rehearsals.

PERFORMERS

The search for suitable performers can be long and involved. You may have to drum up enthusiasm and volunteers for many weeks prior to rehearsals starting. If you have the support of the local council or authority, they may assist with contacting schools, drama clubs and other associations. Never underestimate how long this is going to take. Your search for an ideal two thousand performers may end up with a dedicated group of two hundred keen but not ideal performers, and the same is true about volunteers.

For on-site rehearsals, you may need to allow for a smaller duplicate set of the technical equipment that will be used for the actual show: a smaller sound system, the tower or viewing platform already mentioned, and all the facilities that your performers will require such as mobile toilets, any catering facilities, weather shelter, seating for chaperones, parents or teachers, car parking for performers, paramedics, and any other items specific to your event such as props and staging.

Your choreographer may need a tower or viewing platform in order to be able to see rehearsals clearly.

Make sure there is a clearly indicated signing-in area and somewhere for all the performers to leave coats and bags. It is worth reminding all concerned not to bring valuables on site with them, but inevitably there will be problems and at the end of the day you will have to do a tour of the space to collect lost property.

Many choreographers or directors have a 'three hits and you're out' system for those who continuously miss rehearsals without prior notice. If this is the case, a large sign or signs clearly stating this policy should be prominently displayed. This is often difficult if someone has been ill and you then have the onerous task of explaining to them why they can no longer be involved as they have missed too many rehearsals. It is never easy to explain to performers, however old they may be, that they have missed too many rehearsals and they will be relegated to a walk-on part. The choreographer or director will keep a watch for over-heated performers, and will ensure that there are sufficient rest breaks. They will also check that everyone is wearing sun-block before rehearsals begin.

It is useful to choose a piece of music to serve as the signal for everyone to return to the pitch or field where you are rehearsing, as this is an more efficient way of getting everyone's attention. Choose something lively and up-tempo and easy to recognize. You may want to select some cooling-down music as well, for the break periods.

Watch out for over-keen local journalists. Local newspapers will want to hear about the bad as well as the good on your event, and someone fainting or twisting their ankle can be converted into a headline of 'Performers collapse with heat exhaustion' and 'Children suffer injuries in rehearsals' very easily. Competitions and prizes can keep the interest going during long rehearsal periods, and 'swag' event T-shirts, hats and badges make great prizes for winners and rewards for good attendance.

SITE PREPARATION

With all your meetings successfully completed and the various processes and checks in place, your site should be slowly transforming.

The following will need to be up and running as soon as possible:

- Power.
- Water.
- Mobile toilets.
- Catering.
- Offices.
- Communications.
- Passes for parking, access, catering.
- Parking.
- Security (checking vehicles and protecting equipment left on site).
- Local information (taxis, hotels, fast food delivery if catering stops at a certain time, hospital numbers, times of last trains).
- First aid assistance for load in and build, if necessary.

As on any type of event, the site office will become the centre of attention. If sufficient money is available in your budget then two offices as a minimum, one for crew, deliveries and technical enquiries and one for choreographers and stage managers will ease the pressure and noise. As the event build continues, radios or comms, first aid, and so on, will move into their own areas.

Handy items will be:

- Wipe clean boards for noting phone numbers, contact details, rehearsal calls.
- Pin boards for messages.
- Hook boards for the various keys to offices, equipment, cars.

- Sufficient space and power for radio chargers, phone chargers, laminating machine for passes and anything else specific to your event.

RUNNING THE EVENT

With the addition of audience, stewards, performers, volunteers and everyone else involved on your event, flag raisers, emergency services, and all the crew, you will have a large number of people to deal with on a daily basis. On a large event, be aware that the emergency services will need to plan a rehearsal of the emergency evacuation procedure.

Volunteers and performers will all require accreditation passes and will go through the same process as your crew. You will need to establish an efficient system for collating contact names and addresses, emergency

'If you are using volunteers make sure that they are used, that they are comfortable in their setting, and that any special skill is being used. Brief them clearly and ask for their feedback, don't assume they know what you do. You need to make sure that they have an outdoor kit with them, the right clothes, sun protection, warm clothes, wet weather clothes, comfy shoes and a good book! If they are working away from everyone else then make sure they have food and drink for the day. Finally thank them, you cannot thank volunteers too often and make sure they know that they are appreciated.'

Kerry Peavey, Freelance Sports
Events Manager, Texas, USA

Children rehearsing. You can also just see the pitch markers that guide them to the right spot on the field.

numbers, car registration and so on and you should consider designing a database showing who appears in which routine or number, or what task or duty they perform.

Choreographers and dancers may need additional rehearsals space for mapping out any 'blocking' or choreography prior to going on site.

THE SHOW

Once clearance has been given to start, the show caller will have control of the event, although on large events, they will have to rely on information from members of your team with regards to actions or movements that they cannot see. Various problems will always arise during the event, ranging from people being unable to find their car in a large car park, to accidents and missing children.

The transformation and change of atmosphere as performers move from a quiet rehearsal area off site to the main performance area may come as a culture shock. They may feel swamped by all the technology and numbers of people actually working on the site. After having spent time working closely with a handful of people, choreographers and a couple of stage managers, they find themselves being organized by seemingly battalions of people. A familiarization tour of the site and introduction to the key players will give performers confidence and make them aware of no-go areas and how to find help. The performers should to be introduced to all the members of staff who will be working with them, such as stage managers and dressers, and they should be shown where their props will be stored.

Depending on the size of your event, there may be holding or assembly areas, where performers can wait before making their entrance and specific routes for them to use.

You may have to consider the issue of any security passes needed to move around the site. If the costume has nowhere to hide a bulky pass, you may have to re-think the style of pass given to the performers, especially if the event is to be televised.

LOAD OUT AND DE-BRIEF

The load out on an outdoor event will include a massive tidy-up operation of litter and anything else left on the site. You will be responsible for returning the site to the condition in which you found it. Hopefully the de-brief will be uneventful, although there will almost inevitably be complaints about car parks and mobile facilities. No matter how many times mobile toilets are cleaned, you can guarantee that someone will check them immediately prior to a scheduled cleaning. With regards to car parks, if thousands of cars try to leave the event at the same time, there will inevitably be delays.

OPENING AND CLOSING CEREMONIES FOR SPORTING EVENTS

If you are working on the opening or closing ceremony of a sporting event, for example the Commonwealth or Olympic games, your show script will follow strict guidelines as set out by the relevant organization. In the case of an Olympic event, this will be the IOC.

For example, for Olympic events, there is a set order to be followed: a welcome from the host nation (the entertainment) showing the culture of that nation, raising and lowering of flags, speeches, the entrance of athletes, the entrance of the 'Olympic' torch and the lighting of the flame all have their correct place. Diplomats, politicians or royalty may also be attending, and their arrival will determine the start of the show.

Whilst you may have rehearsed the entertainment section of the event for many weeks, possibly with volunteers standing in as VIPs, it can be very difficult to have a true feeling for the amount of time it takes for thousands of athletes to enter the stadium in the correct order and assemble behind the correct flag and their nation's name sign. The nation's flag will usually be raised on a flag pole as the team comes in to view.

You will have been able to rehearse the flags and name carrying with the volunteers but of course the athletes will only arrive just prior to the ceremony itself. Do not underestimate the number of people managers you will need in the assembly area for the athletes, and bear in mind that some countries by tradition do a whole circuit of the stadium before taking their positions. Some countries have many more competitors and officials parading than others and some enjoy the thrill and cheers from the crowd and join in the fun of the moment. There are military guidelines for how long a parade will take with a stride of a certain length, which is fine for a regimented army but not so helpful when dealing with athletes. As a start, you should allow at least 45 minutes for all the athletes to enter from the marathon gate, make one lap of the track and take their positions. However, it can take up to 60 minutes and your team of stage managers, people movers and choreographers will spend a lot of their time track-side hurrying along athletes who are enjoying the moment a little too much.

It is likely that music will have been especially commissioned for the event and you will probably have 'live' bands to cue as well.

Whilst there is usually plenty of time to rehearse the opening ceremony you will find you will have very few days in which to prepare for the closing ceremony, and probably none at the actual venue, owing to the sporting competitions in the main venue. So you will be back in the 'other' venue, without the buzz and excitement to spur everyone on. This, therefore, by necessity will be a much lower key affair, usually with parades rather than staged items. Because everyone is tired from the opening ceremony you will find that this ceremony is in a way far more stressful as it is difficult to get people to focus on it. If you have a parade of various local community groups, you will have little time to prepare them for the atmosphere and the 'real' venue.

The start of the ceremony will be determined by the last medal presentation ceremonies. Any podium or presentation areas will have to be cleared away before setting up any of the staging elements.

This ceremony, again, is governed by IOC or equivalent rules: you will have speeches, the entrance of the athletes – hopefully a shorter version than at the start of the event, but still with the same mustering problems, and the participants may be very exuberant after their triumphs. You will probably have a video celebrating their achievements, lowering of flags and the official handing over of the flag to the next host nation. You may also have the extinguishing of the 'Olympic' flame.

CARNIVALS, PARADES AND STREET PARTIES

When organizing events like these you will be closely involved with the local community.

With large numbers of crowds watching the parades or carnivals, close liaison with the local council offices, police, and other services will be needed. You will also be working closely with local community leaders representing the cultural mix of the area staging or presenting the event.

Whilst you are searching for participants, you will also be looking for stewards and marshals to work in conjunction with the police to maintain crowd control and safety at an event.

The Battle of Trafalgar, *battle sequence.*

You may need to consider the following:

- Whether you wish to arrange for the various groups, bands and performers to meet with children from the local school.
- Arranging a safe area, if possible, for storing personal belongings.
- Access to toilets and changing facilities.
- Car parking for performers or participants.
- Catering for performers and staff.
- A suitable mustering or assembly point for all the participants and any floats to line up before the start of the parade.
- If the parade does not perform a circuit, arrangements for participants to be collected and returned to the starting point.
- If children will be taking part in the event, ensuring that there are suitable chaperones or group leaders.

It is very useful to arrange a central phone number to be used for any enquiries. As for any other major event, you need to organize first aid, an enquiry tent or point. You should consider whether to use one of the counselling services available to provide pastoral care at open air events. These organizations specialize in helping people who may be at their first event, are by themselves, or have lost their money or their lift home. They are often extremely useful on music or so-called 'folk-festivals'.

When you begin the organization of such an event, you will have to consider transport of instruments and large carnival costumes and you will need clear guidelines about who will be funding these expenses.

7   SPECIFIC EVENTS

FASHION SHOWS

Fast moving and high-pressured, these events have a totally different build-up and process compared to other events.

A fashion show will be driven by the designer on a professional event, who will usually be your source of information on all aspects of the show, covering everything from who will be the models to the running order of the show. The same is true of a charity event, where the models are volunteers and rehearsal time may be at a premium. If you are a stage manager or organizer, you may find the information you need difficult to obtain.

On a professional event, the designer's objectives will be slightly different to your own, as event manager. The designer will want to achieve good press coverage, as well as a great show for the audience of buyers and VIPs. Your start times will be driven by the availability of the models – if they have appeared in other shows on the same day, you will have an anxious time waiting for them to arrive and change. Shows can sometimes begin hours behind schedules because of this, and it can cause a knock-on effect for any shows after yours. There is very little that you can do in this situation, even though you will bear the brunt of all the questions and demands to start the show. If your models have not yet arrived, the designer is unlikely to be willing to begin the show unless the missing models appear way down the running order and the designer is willing to take the risk that they may not arrive in time.

Assuming that your designer is showing in a controlled environment, as part of a regular event, design, backstage requirements and seating will not be a major issue for you. However, if you are staging a charity event, or if your designer wants to use a unique venue, then as for any event there is a process to follow.

THE VENUE

If you, or your designer, have decided on a standard fashion show presentation, with a long runway or catwalk for the models to appear on, your audience may have to sit on tiered seating in order to see. If the audience is seated in rows behind one another and the runway or catwalk is not raised, many members of the audience will be unable to see half of every outfit.

The venue must be long enough to accommodate not only a backstage area for the models, but also provide a large enough area for press photographers at the end of the runway, and any additional seating required for the audience.

When considering space backstage, you will need information on the number of models that will be used, how many changes each model will make during the show, whether a separate make-up and hairdressing area will be required, and whether you will need space for any catering backstage. In addition, you will need to allow for press, cameras, areas where interviews can take place, and anything

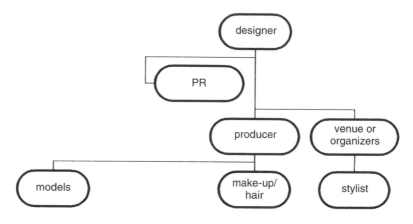

Organization chart for a fashion show.

else that sponsors or others have requested. You will find that privacy is not an issue.

For the front of house, if you are to hand out passes or tickets for your event, table space will be needed for this in your 'foyer'.

If refreshments or a welcome area will be provided for your audience, some space at the entrance to your venue will be needed, along with an area where any displays, press information packs, exhibitions, point of purchase or merchandizing can be sited. Your designer may not think of these issues as a priority at this stage, so it is useful for you to keep in your mind a clear idea of the layout and space that will be required.

If the start of the show is delayed and your designer does not want the audience in and seated, you may have to allow for an area large enough to hold the audience for as long as necessary. Be aware of health and safety regulations governing the capacities of certain areas and the emergency exits for the particular venue. The more whacky or unusual the venue, the more thought you will have to put into these issues, along with the provision of mobile toilets, signage and everything that will transform the space into a 'theatre'.

Pulling the Show Together

Assuming that the models on a professional event are not your responsibility, the build up to the event follows much the same processes outlined in previous chapters.

For a regularly staged event held in one of the international fashion weeks in London, Paris, New York or Milan, the staging will be provided. However you will still have to organize extra items specific to your event, such as:

- Your designer's logo for the set.
- A sign displaying your designer's name and perhaps the title of the collection.
- Additional lighting or special effects.
- The floor covering for the runway.

When organizing a fashion show, you will have fewer formal schedules to prepare than for other events and the meetings will be between you and the designer. On a charity event, you will probably find it more useful to stick to the formal process, with meetings, agendas, schedules and the other processes.

You will probably be more involved in arrangements regarding the audience and invitations than would be normal or usual on any other type of event. You may have to source seating, arrange for names to be displayed on seats, and organize the distribution of 'goody' or gift bags and programmes.

Backstage

For the backstage area, you will need to organize lighting, tables, chairs, hanging rails and possibly refreshments and security. Security may be no more than a team member who checks who has arrived backstage, but the person in charge of security will also have to watch for people coming backstage from the audience uninvited, including members of the press and photographers.

As the preparations for your show progress, a running order will come together. The models make a certain number of 'exits' rather than the usual theatrical 'entrances'. Your designer will take photographs of each model, in every outfit that they will be wearing in the show, and these are placed on a large sheet which will hang on the costume rails next to the outfits. A second set of photographs will be produced with the models' photographs arranged in order of their 'exits', so that you can see who is to come on next and check that what the model is wearing is correct for that 'exit'. This set of photographs usually hangs on the back of the scenery close by where the stage manager or show producer will stand with the designer cuing the models on. You should not expect to see this version until the show day.

Even at a charity event, it is useful to produce similar sheets as these as they will be a source of information for your models and any helpers and help to prevent any confusion.

Your designer may well have chosen music for the event; however you should always have some additional music available as applause and delays can mean that the music planned runs out very quickly.

Of course, as for any event some form of

communication between lighting, sound and yourself will be required.

Show Day

On the day of the show, it is usually advisable to start by checking that backstage is set up correctly. Review all the obvious areas, such as seating, lighting, make-up, hairdressing, mirrors, costume rails, running orders and anything else specific to your show. Remember to check that you have a table available for you to place your running order.

You will have organized logos, signage and special effects for the stage. You should ensure that your runway is protected from foot prints and dust during rehearsals, and if it needs cleaning, you will have the usual problem of making sure that it will be dry for your show. On most professional events, the organizers will have ensured that the runway is painted freshly for each show. They will usually provide

Press and photographers

Just as your side of the show is coming together, press and photographers will seemingly perform the impossible by seeing how many marks they can put down in the smallest space dead centre at the end of the runway, to protect their spot for their ladder, camera, or for them to stand. Discussions can get quite heated as they are all fighting for that front page exclusive shot of one of the supermodels or any incident in your show, which could potentially earn them a fortune. After the fight to win their space, the ground will be covered in white tape, ink-marked with the names of all the internationally renowned publications and you will still be amazed that they will all fit in to that space when they return for the show.

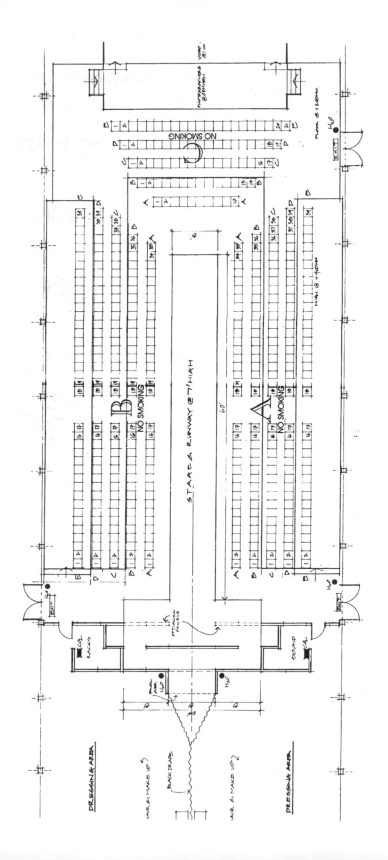

Ground plan showing layout for Philip Treacy at London Fashion Week.

plastic sheeting to lay over the runway to protect it. You may wish to place marks on the runway to indicate stopping or turning positions for the models.

During the show, your role may be split between the foyer or reception area, the audience and backstage. Seating VIPs and ensuring that everyone has arrived will be a priority, before you go backstage and see what the state of play is with models. Even if you are working with an experienced PR company, you will need to keep appraised of what is happening in the audience.

If the press have invaded the backstage area inevitably there will come a moment when you or your designer will ask for them all to leave. With a crowd backstage it can be impossible to see how many models you have, and the noise level can become unbearable. It is still a show, a performance, and there does need to be an attempt of calm before it starts.

Once you have clearance for the show to start, you must remember to inform all team members in the front of house areas that the show is ready to begin.

Based backstage with the designer, your main role will usually be to tell the lighting operator which model is on next. Models will be handled by dressers and are usually very experienced at getting themselves to the right place ready for their next 'exit'. If a model is late and the designer has not noticed, inform the designer as soon as possible to allow the designer to change the running order as appropriate. Do not attempt to get involved in this.

Traditionally the last exit before the curtain call is a bridal outfit or similar, then the designer and the whole cast of models enter, take the applause and return backstage. The clothes will be packed by the designer's team and returned to their base. As with any event, do not forget to check the front of house and collect any display material remaining.

European Union Youth Orchestra, at the Berlin Philharmonie, 2000, under Vladimir Ashkenazy. The soloists are Dam-Jensen and Birgit Remmert. Photo: Kal Biemart.

CAR LAUNCHES

Whilst there is no 'standard' car launch they are all likely to follow roughly the same format. If the manufacturer has a new model to launch out there may be as many as three different presentations:

- Presentation to the worldwide dealer network.
- Press launch.
- Internal presentations, 'family days', and sales presentations.

*Freelander Launch,
Spain, 1997.*

You may also be involved in a pre-launch event, where selected dealers are shown round the factory whilst the vehicle still has a code name and is not yet ready for launch. These events have the highest security, with no cameras or mobile phones allowed. Visitors are usually asked to remove all jewellery or other metal objects such as watches to avoid damage to the vehicles as they are shown round.

A basic launch event may begin on day one with a presentation session, with an introduction to the vehicle and its main selling points and new features. There will be a 'reveal' of the vehicle, which is usually a spectacular affair.

Dealer information meetings are held during the day and a welcome evening meal is usually arranged in the town where the launch is being held. On day two there may be a 'ride and drive', where everyone gets a chance to travel in the new vehicle. Depending on the size of the company and where the launch is being held, there may be another celebration meal on day two and also some smaller meetings. On day three that particular group or 'wave' of delegates departs.

These programmes can run for some weeks. They are very expensive and there is huge competition to upstage rival manufacturers with not only the vehicle but with the standard of entertainment provided. The competition amongst event/production companies to acquire and retain vehicle manufacturers or 'car companies' is cut-throat, as these events are extremely valuable financially. Secrecy, as has already been mentioned is paramount, and clients may insist that event companies do not also work for other rival car companies.

Family Days

These shows are completely different to the events held for the dealers. The same short show may be presented up to five times a day over a period of a few weeks. Such events are usually open to all employees who have worked on the vehicle, together with their families. They are seen as a 'thank you' to the staff and a morale booster.

Press Launches

The press launch for a car may sometimes be held at the major car shows around the world, for example Geneva, New York, Detroit, and Birmingham. These are very important events and the finish, quality and content of any stands must be immaculate.

Additional Information

Whatever the type of car launch, an infinite amount of attention to detail will always be required. Teams of cleaners and specialist finishers will work on presenting the cars at their best. On a continuous ride and drive programme these teams will work overnight so that each wave of delegates drives a car that looks like new.

The 'brand' or the 'marque' as it is sometimes known, refers to the company name, the logo and what that name or image means to people. For example if you think of 'Rolls-Royce', you probably have an immediate understanding of what the brand stands for, and the sort of people that would own or want to own one of these cars. The smaller family economy cars work the hardest to develop their brand image and are continuously re-assessing it. They will work hard on brand association and lifestyle images that refer to or relate to their brand. When pitching for one of these lucrative events, it is crucial that you have an understanding of their brand and all the brand associations involved with the new model.

Special editions of existing models are often brought out in the summer, and new vehicles are usually launched in the autumn, although this is not always the case. Before a new model is launched, most companies will stage events or run an advertising campaign, in order to 'shift metal', that is, to clear old models off the dealers' forecourts to make way for the new vehicles. The dealers will often stage customer events, but these do not usually involve event companies.

WORKING WITH ORCHESTRAS

There are various types and size of orchestras. These range from a symphony orchestra, which is the largest, through to a chamber orchestra, and all the variations in between of string quartets, wind quartets and so on.

The photo on page 85 shows the EUYO (the European Union Youth Orchestra), which can be made up of 142 players. Aged 14–23 years and drawn from all the EU Member States, the age range and the different languages spoken by the different members of the orchestra bring their own challenges and opportunities.

Musicians will practise anywhere they can and every day. You will often find a peaceful afternoon in your hotel is accompanied by the sounds of a variety of instruments practising. This enthusiasm and dedication will rub off on even the most cynical organizer as you discover that by choosing to move your office to the back of the concert hall, even the most mundane jobs such as rooming, lists, plane tickets and other administrative tasks can be accompanied by your own personal symphony orchestra as they rehearse.

All orchestras will have similar requirements and you should be aware of the following.

Space
Allow 1.5 m^2 per person. This is to allow for someone sitting, with perhaps a 'cello and a 'T Bar' (this is the bar that a cellist will use to prevent the spike at the bottom of the instrument from slipping). If the musicians are too tightly packed then there will not be enough 'bowing' room, in other words the members of the string section will not be physically able to move their bows as they play without knocking other players.

Chairs and high stools
The orchestra will require armless chairs to perform on (if they do not provide their own chairs), and the double bass players and

OPPOSITE: Jodie Kidd, for Philip Treacy at London Fashion Week (autumn/winter 98/99). Photo: Robert Fairer.

sometimes the percussionists will require high or bar stools to sit on.

Risers
The orchestra will use risers for the back row, which may possibly be percussion, or any of the brass or wind section who need to be raised in order to see the conductor.

Sound baffles and other items
The orchestra may bring with them Perspex or other sound baffles that sit between two rows of players, for example in front of the wind or brass sections. The orchestra may also take the conductor's podium or rostrum with them on tour, together with a stool for rehearsals or long performances.

Lighting
Members of the orchestra will usually have lights on their music stands, and will also need stage lighting in order to see the conductor. An electrician should be available in order to move any lanterns that are shining in any of the musicians' eyes or for any other adjustments that need to be made.

Dressing rooms
Usually separate dressing rooms will be required for the conductor, any soloists, and the leader of the orchestra, and then as many rooms as are available for men and women. You may need to consider storage issues for instrument cases and travelling cases (the wooden boxes in which double basses, some 'cellos, harps and the percussion will travel).

Orchestra staff
Three members of staff may accompany the larger orchestras.

- Librarian: responsible for all the music scores, making any musical changes to each score, setting out and collecting the music on the day of the performance, and maintaining the orchestra's library.

- Stage manager: responsible for loading and unloading instruments and setting out music stands, staging requirements, lighting and so on.
- Orchestra or tour manager: responsible for all travel, and other administrative systems, and acts as a main point of contact.

Travelling

Many players prefer to take their instruments with them rather than put them on the orchestra's wagon or lorry. If the orchestra is flying, you will need to discover whether the hold is pressurized or not, or whether there are seats on the aircraft for their instruments. The musicians will be concerned because temperature or pressure changes in the hold could potentially damage their very valuable instruments. If there are seats booked for their instruments (this may sometimes be done for the 'cellos), make sure that the flight crew do not waste time trying to find 'Mr and Mrs Cello', when there are instruments in those seats.

Additional Information

Some terminology is specific to an orchestra.

- Seating rehearsal: this rehearsal will usually take place on the day of a concert or performance and apart in addition to checking the layout and lighting, they will also perform a sound check.
- Desks: this refers to the stand where two players sit; for example front desks and back desks.
- Leader: the leader of the orchestra is the second in command to the conductor and sits at the first desk of the 'fiddles' or first violins, and sits on the right hand side or the side nearest to the audience. The leader of each section sits at the front desk for that

section in the same position, on the right as you are standing behind them or on the left from the conductor's viewpoint. The orchestra not only takes the musical lead from the leader but will take its bow or stand for the conductor's entrance by following the leader. The leader will also indicate applause from the orchestra by tapping the music stand with the bow, in appreciation of the conductor or a soloist.

- Tuning: literally, when the members of the orchestra tune their instruments. They will take an A from the oboe. But, there are many different 'A' frequencies depending on where your orchestra is from, and if you are arranging for the hire and therefore the tuning of a piano for the orchestra, then the tuner will need to know what frequency the orchestra tunes to.

If you are touring with an orchestra, then some contacts in the towns that you are visiting will be useful. You may be asked for details of suppliers of strings, bow repairers, drum repairers, suppliers of new drum sticks, and any other instrument repairers or shops that may be open out-of-hours. In extremis, opera houses and theatres may be able to help you.

GARDEN FÊTES AND SIMILAR COMMUNITY EVENTS

One of the most important types of events, and probably the most common, is the community or local event. Planned months in advance as either an annual event, a fundraising event or just to bring the community together, these are an important part of life, all over the world.

The general processes stated in this book apply to this type of event as well. However there is of course one main difference: the organizers and all the participants, stall holders, stewards, caterers and so on, will usually

The EUYO in 1986, Madrid. This photo shows the size of a full symphony orchestra.

all be volunteers, giving up their spare time to give something back to the community purely for the fun of it.

The Brief, or Creative Stage

You will probably have a very experienced committee that has worked on events in your town or village for many years. If you find yourself at the helm of a new event there will always be people with relevant experience who will underpin you and be incredibly valuable. This is one area where age and experience

really do count. You may have a set format of, for example, venue and layout. In certain circumstances you may well have started planning the next year's event before the current event has started.

Over the years a tried and trusted formula will have been found that appeals to the target audience and that your team of volunteers can easily handle – at some point someone will say that it is 'dull, predictable, that it is missing something'! Your brainstorming session may well be held during one of your committee meetings and you have a lot of advantages compared with event organizers pitching against many companies for an event: you know your target audience very well and you also know what your team is capable of managing. If you haven't worked with volunteers before, you may not be aware that you do have one huge disadvantage: your volunteers are just that, volunteers. They are under no obligation to turn up on the day and people do get sick, go on holiday or move out of the area. Your brainstorming will have to take this into consideration as well.

Before you start adding new or untried elements to your event you need to take every new element into consideration: who will organize it, where will it go and, most obvious of all, why do you all think you need it? Rather than add new things to your event, perhaps you might better stick to altering some of the existing elements:

- Which elements have not been so financially viable?
- What has not been so popular?
- What has been difficult to staff or manage on the day?
- Were any elements too weather reliant?
- Were they aimed at too specific an age group, which maybe has changed or moved on over the years?
- Is there a change to the layout that would add a little more interest?
- Did your income match everyone's expectations and does the budget need to be altered in any way?

WI home produce market.

Of course, for everything you cut or alter there will always be repercussions, financial or otherwise, and for an event that relies heavily on the goodwill of the volunteer organizers any change may be better put on hold and planned-for over a few years. For example, you may never have had the need to draw up a plan of your event, but altering the layout might call for one to be drawn up for the first time in years. It could give you a new perspective on the layout and allow for some fresh thinking.

When you do reach your decision on the date and content for your event remember to go through the staffing:

• Ticket sellers.
• Car park attendants.
• Stewards.
• Stall holders.
• Cash handlers and what you are going to do with the money on site, security, and so on.
• First Aid and help from any emergency services.

You won't need to fix these at this stage but it is good to go through the numbers and the names of people who have specific responsibilities and their availability this time around.

Advertising and marketing

You have done this event every year and everyone knows about it, but do they know why you are doing it this year? Maybe there is a special cause or you have a guest of honour opening the event. This could be the year that you create new street signs advertising it, perhaps your changes could be something worth telling your local press about. If you need more volunteers from outside your community, or would like to draw in a bigger crowd than usual, then getting in front of a reporter at the earliest possible opportunity will help your cause. Make sure you have a press release to give them, so they have something to take

away with them or indeed something that you can fax to them to interest them in your event. Bear in mind the following points when preparing your press release:

• It should be on one side of A4 only.
• The heading should state clearly the title of the event with the date and time.
• Your opening sentence is going to be the one that attracts the attention – perhaps the statement that a celebrity will be opening your fête this year.
• List the attractions.
• State the ticket price.
• Give timings.
• Include volunteer enquiry details and contact number
• Make sure there is a contact name and number for press enquiries.

A journalist used to give talks at the Central Office for Information and regularly started his talk by placing two five-ream boxes of paper on the table in front of him and then asked the attendees if they knew what these boxes represented. The answer was that it was the number of press releases a newspaper editor receives, daily. There is no guarantee that yours will attract any attention: a follow-up phone call may help, but always give a reason for calling, perhaps to tell them something else or new about the event that was not on the press release.

The Preparation

You will be having regular meetings about your event and probably there will not be that much to report, but it is essential that any information is distributed to all the team leaders or whatever you decide to call the people responsible for the various sections of your event.

By making clear divisions on the event you can give people ownership of certain areas and make it possible for you to take an overview and 'float' in case of emergencies. A genuine sense of ownership is very important on any event and will enable your volunteers to feel that they have significant input and that they are a crucial member of the team.

There are things to be aware of and to check that the 'team leader' or whoever has in hand:

- Licences – do you need a lottery or raffle licence, an alcohol or beverages licence? Have you allowed enough time to apply for any specific requirements for your region?
- Have you told relevant public departments about your event: Police, Fire Brigade and Ambulance Service?
- Do you need to do a courtesy letterbox drop to the neighbouring houses reminding them about the event, where they can park, apologizing for inconvenience and noise?
- 'Never assume' applies to these events too. Do you need to check that the venue or space is available? Even if it has been for the past fifty years, remember to check, confirm and hold any meetings well in advance, so that there can be no misunderstandings.
- Volunteers – do you have enough and are all the usual people in place, briefed and happy with their role? Do you have a health and safety officer, a site officer and anything else specific to your event?
- If someone is 'missing' this year are you fully aware of what they used to do, what area they covered and who is replacing them?
- Remember to thank everyone, continuously. They have given up their spare time, which needs acknowledgement. And you cannot do it without them!
- Have you an allocation in your spend fund that allows for some 'TLC' for your volunteers – ice cream, tea and coffee, lunch?

The Days Before the Event

Hopefully you have the weather you are hoping for and the event is a few days away. You now need to check that all your 'team' – the volunteers, stall holders, and so on – have a schedule and know what to do, and that they know what the contingency plan is for bad weather or even cancellation. You will probably have issued an 'emergency' phone number so that anyone unable to attend on the day can give as much notice as possible. Your schedule will probably include some of the following:

- Site preparation.
- Distribution and erection of signage.
- Any collections and deliveries.
- Briefing session for stewards.
- Emergency evacuation briefing for stall or marquee holders.
- An outline of the day's events.
- A list of the 'team leaders' for each section.
- A 'what to do' section for lost property, lost children, loss of power/water, sudden change in weather and the like.
- What to do after the event: litter patrol, cash collection, removal of signage and so on.

The Day of the Event

However early everyone has to get up, and to a certain extent whatever weather you wake up to, there will always be a sense of achievement and an adrenalin rush, which will see everyone through.

How you judge the success of your event will be specific to your event and your past experience. But there will always be 'crises' to deal with – lost children, missing stewards or stalls – but with good communication on the day and a sense of humour all these things are usually dealt with quickly. Remember to keep a tight hold on the schedule, especially if you have VIPs arriving to open your event.

One of your main duties though will be one of encouragement and maintaining an air of

Where something more than just a First Aid box is needed, St John Ambulance can be very helpful.

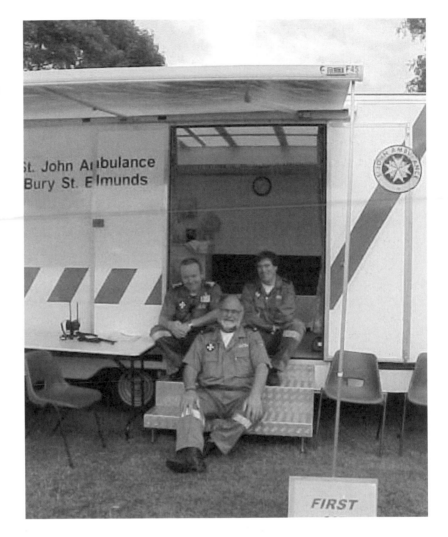

calm when hearing reports of 'disasters'. Hopefully there won't be any true disasters, merely small problems or challenges that are easily solved but that to over-anxious and caring members of your team may seem insurmountable.

Your task list at the end of the event will consist of clearing the site, thanking everyone and anything else that is relevant to your event. Hopefully you will have had time to enjoy yourself as well!

The De-Brief

It would be marvellous if your version of the de-brief was to congratulate everyone on a great event, hard work and announcing the money raised as a result of all their efforts.

There may be issues to address that can be looked at over the ensuing months ready for the next event. As your meetings are likely to be well-minuted, then the history of any successes, failures or problems will be easily accessible for everyone. But, keep your own notes, anything that will act as an *aide-memoire* for the next year. For example, why things happened, the actions or events that led up to any unusual situations, and how people managed in their areas. This may seem an obvious thing to do, but it is really easy to imagine that you will remember it all in detail a year later, and that is not always the case.

After everything has been discussed, challenged and noted, hopefully everyone will be agreed that they have had fun!

GYMKHANAS

Often seen as the poor relation to the 'proper' horse events to which they are often attached, these entertaining events require careful planning along with experienced help. If you find yourself in the great position of organizing one of these 'children's' events then you will be working on one of the most enjoyable events around. Usually set up after the main competitions of the day, you will need a well-trained team to help you set up in time and to maintain the audience's interest. If you are fortunate enough to be staging a stand-alone event, then your task is a little easier.

To get expert help on board you should probably contact one of the many international branches of The Pony Club. They have a list of experts and helpers to advise and guide, not only on general rules for the competitions but also, vitally, for health and safety at the event.

The Venue
This may be a sectioned-off field to the side of the main arena, you may be setting up on the main arena, or if you are lucky then you will have the luxury of finding a willing landowner who will let you have the use of a field for the day. The last instance means that you have a clear schedule ahead of you to organize the layout and the set-up for all the events. A few points to remember:

- The size of the field or arena will vary, but you should aim for one approximately $85 \times 50m$ ($280 \times 160ft$) wide.
- You should aim to have a clearly marked entrance to the arena and a separate exit in order that young, inexperienced riders and ponies won't get confused, nor will the judges and stewards!
- At one end by the two marked entrances/ exits there will be a collecting ring, where the riders wait to be called.
- Of course, with ponies come horse trailers, trucks and cars that need to be directed to a large-enough area away from the arena and collecting ring, so as not to cause a traffic jam of people and ponies.
- You will need paramedics on site and, if you have a large event, then a vet should be on standby.
- You will need a practice area for the riders and ponies to warm up in. This has to be away from the parking area for safety.
- Wherever you choose, you have to ensure that there is room for access to the site for trailers, horseboxes and so on.
- There must be shade and water available.
- You need to ensure there is weather cover or wind cover for judges.
- An area for mobile toilets must be provided.

Preparing and Planning
Assuming you have found your venue then the date of the event, supply of volunteers, cost of entry for spectators, the rules for entry for the competitors, costs of each event and what to do about late entries all have to be decided. You will need a host of experienced experts:

- Judges.
- Collecting-ring stewards.

*OPPOSITE: **All dressed up for a gymkhana.***

- Arena party stewards, who set up equipment between events.
- Caterers.
- Announcer.
- Car park attendants.
- Paramedics.
- Vet.
- Clear-up team for litter.
- Treasurer.
- Prizes – rosettes, etc
- Print and publicity
- Insurance, public liability, contractual liability and so on.

Equipment

You should take advice from the local governing body on jumps, layout and equipment, but you will also need mobile toilets and marquees for catering, First Aid and the announcer. You will also need a public address system for announcements of events, winners and the like.

If you are in any doubt about anyone's experience then you must check, especially if this is your first event. Discovering that you are all first timers when faced with the first runaway pony is not going to be a great moment, and could be very dangerous.

The Build-Up to the Event

The longer you have to prepare for this, the better, of course. If you have a three-month lead-in then this will guarantee you good advertising, maximum entrants and good volunteers to help you with the event proper.

Two months before: if you are in contact with a local organization such as The Pony Club, then you will have invitations to the judges to send out, as well as all the equipment to source and order.

One month before: your advertising can be very cheap by printing out leaflets that are displayed in pet-food stores, tack shops and, if possible, at other rallies or gymkhanas leading up to your event.

The week before: all you volunteers and competitors will need a confirmation of timings, a schedule of sorts, maps and any other information that you have not already sent out. For example, confirmation of dress code, emergency phone numbers, late arrivals, where to park and so on.

The night before: you will be hoping to set up your arena the night before your event, and your mobile toilets and any catering will possibly arrive the night before as well. Marking out the site clearly with stakes or poles and signs will prevent any misunderstandings if you are not immediately available the next morning when the first horse box arrives.

The Event Proper

If you have never been involved with this type of event before, the emphasis is on enjoyment but with quite a lot of discipline, from the turnout of the rider to the kit inspection before the event starts. Health and safety for both horse and rider is key at this sort of event, and the kit inspection is vital to ensure that no-one is in any danger. Your selected experts will be watching for what type of boots or shoes that the rider is wearing and, of course, that they are wearing the correct sort of protective headgear.

Whatever events you select, the skill will be in changing the layout of the arena and assembling the teams or individual riders swiftly enough to maintain everyone's interest and attention.

If you are unlucky enough to have bad weather this will only dampen everyone's enthusiasm a little bit, and if you have provided the competitors with the right information then they should have with them waterproofs to wear when they are competing.

Some of the Pony Club Events

Aunt Sally
Ball and Bucket
Ball and Cone
Balloon Bursting
Bottle Race
Canter, Trot and Walk
Egg and Spoon Race
Fishing Race
Jelly Baby Gobble
Litter Race
Musical Mats
Potato Race

Details of these events can be obtained from The Pony Club around the world.

After the Event

Your main priority will be to clear the site and return it to the owner in a good state of repair. Whatever de-brief you decide to have, thank-you letters to organizers, judges, volunteers and the site owner will be one of your first actions.

Hopefully you will have made enough money to cover the hire of any equipment and be able to allocate some of the profits to the next event.

EXHIBITIONS

If you are organizing an exhibition, then whether the exhibitors are part of the client company or are external you will need to provide them with basic information in order for them to inform you of their requirements:

Taking a jump.

- They will want to know the size of their pod, or display area, and the 'footprint' – the size that they can use.
- Power supply.
- Any height restrictions.
- Weight-loading restrictions if the stand has a false floor.
- Build time allowed.
- Basic schedule.
- Additional costs: power, labour, entertaining.
- Minimum/maximum number of staff for safety.
- Restrictions to size of any mountings or advertising boards, logos and so on.
- Fire safety/health and safety requirements.
- If it is a corporate event, any colour/style requirements.

You may be responsible for producing banners and posters for exhibitor's stands, and you must tell everyone what the deadline is for their 'copy' (the content displayed on these).

Your administration process – contact reports, flow charts and budgets – will follow most of the event process. Contracts and payments will apply not only to suppliers but also to exhibitors for their stand; and there will be a technical rider to adhere to on both sides. You may also have print and display deadlines as a separate warning or information document for everyone, including schedules, names of staff manning the stand and any unusual requirements for the stand.

Points to Watch

Unlike a show or presentation scenario where people only see one side of the event, if your stand is open on three sides or the audience can access all sides, then the finish is crucial.

Cables, lights, and any other 'feed' to the stand have to be co-ordinated with the stand, meet HSE requirements and be finished to a very high standard. In other words, it should be possible to walk around it without seeing gaffer tape, bags, plugs and sockets, cables or anything else that would ruin the finish, or be a trip or other hazard from the HSE viewpoint.

Working on an exhibition is hard work for the staff manning the stand and also for anyone who may not be used to having face-to-face contact with the public. You have to be prepared to be an information point, deal with lost people or children, lost property and any other enquiry, whilst manning the stand for your company and keeping a watchful eye that nothing disappears from it.

8   ROLES AND RESPONSIBILITIES

From the moment that you have won your first major event, suddenly there will be teams of people to employ, organize and communicate with.

A.V. operator

(Also called a technician.) The A.V. operator works with the available technology to provide visual support for speakers, and will be responsible for the projectors and all equipment associated with this aspect of the event.

Account director

The account director will usually work closely with a client to develop an understanding of the client's communication issues and wants. However, the account director may not necessarily take a hands-on role when it comes to organizing an event. The account director may often be the client's main point of contact at the event company.

Designer

Working closely with your creative team, the designer will by necessity have a close understanding of the client's image, brand and messaging. The sole responsibility of the design team may be the 3D aspects of the event, or it may also work on all the other design elements such as print, signage, and any theming of external elements of the event.

Draughtsperson

Working closely with the designer, the draughtsperson may be responsible for construction plans, site plans, and keeping all these up-to-date with any changes. The draughtsperson will work closely with scene builders and other construction workers.

Executive producer

(Often called a senior producer.) The executive producer is usually a very experienced member of the team, who will oversee the work of the producer and the team as a whole, but not necessarily take a hands-on role. Sometimes an executive producer may become involved with the event as the result of a request from the client in order to ensure continuity over a series of events, or to ease in the introduction of a new producer to the client.

Health and safety manager

The health and safety manager will be the main contact for any safety issues or regulations regarding the safety of any structures erected, working conditions both indoors and outside, hours of work, suitability of venues and so on.

Lighting designer

The role of the lighting designer may be undertaken by a member of your electrics team. The lighting designer will be responsible

> 'A sense of humour is essential along with comfortable shoes!'
>
> *Emma Chesters,*
> *Freelance Logistics Manager, UK*

for ensuring that enough lamps or lanterns are ordered and supplied for your event, overseeing the placing of the lights and working to create whatever effects are necessary. They will work closely with the producer and or show caller to 'plot' or record the various lighting states.

Local ground agent

The local ground agent will be a very important person for you or your logistics manager, providing local knowledge of hotels, venues, transport, crew, entertainment and local traditions, culture and language.

Logistics manager

A meticulous organizer, flexible and creative, a logistics manager can expect to be involved in budgets, delegate registration (including web design and intranet and internet use), delegate badging, food and beverage, accommodation, transportation, evening events, people movement, hostesses, partner programmes (events organized for partners of delegates attending events) and meeting room usage. The logistics manager will not be daunted by the need to send a list of 100 room changes to the event hotel, and dealing politely and professionally with a delegate who does not appreciate that the one little change requested is possibly the two-hundredth such request that the logistics team has received that day. The logistics team

OPPOSITE: *'Lord Nelson' and a powder boy,* **The Battle of Trafalgar,** *West Wycombe Park, for the National Trust's centenary.*

are also used to doing room drops in the middle of the night distributing welcome packs, programmes and urgent messages for delegates.

Merchandizing manager

Merchandizing managers are more usually involved in outdoor events. The merchandizing manager will be responsible for the sale of T-shirts, programmes, and various memorabilia for the event. The merchandizing manager will usually also be responsible for the staff who will sell the goods.

Model maker

Working with the 3D designer, a model maker will produce a model of the event, exhibition, or set, for reference for your client or to be used by scenic constructors or others on the construction team.

Producer

The producer is the co-ordinator or organizer of the event, and possibly also the creator of

> 'In a logistics manager's little black book you are likely to find:
>
> Ground agents around the world.
> Hotels and conference centres.
> Caterers.
> Coach companies.
> Limo hire companies.
> Air charter companies.
> Furniture hire companies.
> Badging companies.
> Web designers.
> Host's agencies.
> Entertainers.'
>
> *Emma Chesters,*
> *Freelance Logistics Manager, UK*

the event. The producer will be responsible for ensuring all elements of the event meet the client's and the company's expectations, within budget and on time, and will work closely with logistics and the production manager to produce budgets and schedules. The producer must be a team leader and a good communicator. Producers may be responsible for scripts, schedules and may have to act as show caller on smaller events. During run-throughs and the event or show proper, the producer will hand over the reigns to the show caller.

Production manager

The production manager will be responsible to the producer or work alongside the producer to ensure that the technical elements of the event meet the client's and the company's expectations and are delivered on time and within budget. The production manager will be involved in the production of budgets and schedules, alongside the producer and logistics manager. The production manager may also be the crew, transport and site boss. Production managers will also be expected to advise and guide designers and producers on the latest technology available.

Project co-ordinator

Usually a graduate or trainee, the project co-ordinator's role is often a first point of entry for would be producers. Working closely with the producer, offering administration support, project co-ordinators may also have their own areas of responsibility, for example organizing exhibitions and gala dinners, or overseeing the production of the invitations and other printed material for on the event.

Rigging

Also called rigging crew, they are responsible for hanging or suspending any parts of the technical elements of the event from lighting bars or truss, to signage or banners. On some events they may also operate equipment which is off the ground.

Security

The security team may be in-house security, or performing ushers or steward's duties on an outdoor event. Their duties will vary from event to event, but they will be your audience's first point of contact for information and help on some events. The security team may be responsible for car parks, patrolling perimeters, 'guarding' the stage or sensitive areas and monitoring security passes and radios or communications.

Show caller

Usually experienced in the theatre, where they are also called a DSM. The main duties of the show caller will start with marking up a show script with all lighting, sound, visual, scenic elements and people movements, or cues. The show caller will work closely with the producer, sound operator, lighting designer and others to ensure that all information is shown in the script at the exact moment that it should happen. They will also keep all scripts up-to-date, with their own (the master copy) left usually on the podium or lectern in case the auto-Q fails. The show caller should ensure that all departments are informed of any major changes, as necessary, and this can prove to be a full time task. Working on rehearsals, giving the cues over headsets to all the various departments, the show manager should ideally be a calm, clear communicator. Show managers do not usually work on the load-in or load out, although they may be used on gala dinners or other parts of the event where lighting or sound cues occur. On site, there is a subtle shift of power from the producer to the show caller. There can only be one 'boss' and as the show caller knows exactly when potentially dangerous or unusual things will happen on stage, including black outs or scenery movements, then for health and safety reasons there must only be one voice giving the cues.

Site manager

The site manager is another technical manager who may work alongside a production or technical manager but with responsibilities for the site rather than the event content. The site manager may be the main point of contact for site conversion and the placing of various backstage elements such as offices and catering. The main point of contact for deliveries and movement and placement of vehicles on site will usually be the site manager. In addition, the site manager may also be a crew boss for site staff.

Software producer

This is a role which is likely to change considerably as technology evolves and develops. The software producer will usually work with speakers and technicians to produce the visual elements for the presentation. They will be responsible for making sure that all speakers have the same style or design of backgrounds, colours and logos. Software producers may or may not also work on the video elements as well.

Sound operator or designer

This is primarily a technical role, but aspects of this role can also be quite creative. The sound operator will be responsible for all the equipment required in order to allow the audience to hear the speakers and all other elements of the event. The sound operator will have a wide knowledge and experience of the use of microphones and sound balance.

Stage manager

It is relatively uncommon for a stage manager to be involved in events, but if present the stage manager's role will be to cue on speakers or to run the backstage areas, especially if there are significant movements of people or other elements of the production or event. Stage managers are usually experienced in theatre work.

Stewards or ushers

The stewards may be working with or for the security team or be employed by the logistics team. They will be 'meeters and greeters' at the entrance to the event, and may show people to their seats or be stationed at various points around your venue as a source of information. The stewards play a vital role in any emergency procedure or evacuation procedure.

Transport manager

The transport manager is responsible for the movement of vehicles on site, parking and access and any necessary documents or paperwork if inter-continental travel is necessary. The transport manager may also be responsible for obtaining car parking passes for the crew and organizing crew mini-buses between venues and hotels; however the transport manager is not usually responsible for air travel apart from possibly arranging airfreight.

Video producer

The video producer will work with the producer and client to produce any videos or filmed elements. Video producers will be responsible for their own crew, and for monitoring budgets, delivery, and so on.

SAMPLE LAYOUT OF AN INCOME-BASED BUDGET

INCOME
Capacity: 3,000
Tickets: 2,000 @ £18.00

less
Tickets – complimentary
Tickets – family concessions
Tickets for sponsors – based on contract
Credit card fees

Break-even set at 65% or less.

Additional Income
Hospitality packages
Programme sales 1 to 3
Catering and concessions
Merchandising
Sponsorship

EXPENDITURE
Performers
Fees
Costumes
Wigs
Make-up
Travel
Accommodation

Fees
Artistic team, director, designer etc
Venue hire
Advertising, PR, print

Technical
Lighting
Sound
Staging
Design
Transport
Props
Mobile facilities, loos, offices,
Site requirements – water, power fencing,
Security – stewards, car park attendants
Signage

GLOSSARY

Account manager A person who works closely with the client and is responsible for assessing the client's needs in relation to the event.

Accreditation A security check system used by various organizations that allows for the identification of any people who may be regarded as potential 'risk' elements prior to them arriving on site.

Auto-Q A system whereby the speakers' scripts are presented to them on special glass or on a monitor that only they (and not the audience) can see, via an operator who follows the speaker's presentation.

Border A piece of scenery or fabric suspended across the stage or performance area that hides lanterns, or the upper part of the stage, from the audience.

Brainstorm Brainstorming: a concerted intellectual treatment of a problem by discussing spontaneous ideas about it.

Brief The client's description of the event or show that is required.

Budget An estimate of the cost of the event, before the event is finalized and accurate quotes are supplied.

Build This literally refers to building any elements of the event or show. Usually referred to as 'the build' it can include all the time prior to the first rehearsal.

Bumper slide Also called a 'holding slide'. This is used as part of the presentation, and usually includes the event logo on it. It may be displayed between speakers or as a stand-by slide.

Cabaret style This refers to the layout of seating for an event: tables with chairs set around them, with a gap at the edge facing the stage or presenter.

Camera left This is the side of the stage that is on the audience's or viewers' left. In theatrical terms this would be 'stage right', in other words, on the right of the performers as they face the audience.

Camera right This is the side of the stage that is on the audience's or viewers' right. In theatrical terms this would be 'stage left', in other words, on the left of the performers as they face the audience

Cans Also called 'headsets'. Used for communication during rehearsals or at an event.

Client facing May refer to either the finish of a document, in other words a document that is finished to the highest standard as opposed to a more plain document for internal use only. Alternatively, a person may also be described as 'client facing'.

Confidentiality agreement   Similar to a non-disclosure agreement, issued by companies and clients to protect information on their products.

Comfort monitor   A monitor or monitors set either side of where the speaker is presenting that shows the speaker what is happening on the screen behind: the 'slides', video and so on.

Comms   An abbreviation of 'communications'. This can refer to headsets, radios, cell phones or any other method used on site for communication.

Cost to client   The amount, including any mark-up or commission, charged to the client on any of the event's costs.

Creds presentation   A first meeting with a potential client where a sales person or new business person presents their company, including an introduction to what they do and who they are, to the client.

Cues or Qs   A selected moment when a light, sound, a scenic or people change, or a movement occurs.

Cue light or Q light   Usually placed on the lectern, this is a button that the speakers can press to indicate to any operator that they are ready to change slides or any other item, as appropriate. It can also refer to a cue light box placed in the wings showing a red warning light indicating that the operator or performer should 'stand by' and a green light to indicate that whatever is about to happen (for example an entrance or movement of scenery) should 'go' (that is, happen).

Dead   A 'dead' is a theatrical expression used to denote the height or mark for a hanging piece, drape or scenic element. It refers to the mark that the operator makes on it to show where it has to be for that particular moment in the event, as in 'Mark the dead there please'. However it can also refer to something such as a prop that is no longer used, as in 'that's dead'.

De-brief   An analysis of the event at a meeting, discussing any points that were unusual, successful or incorrect.

Deck   A theatrical expression for the floor of the stage. Many of these expressions come from the theatre and derive from the terms used by the out-of-work sailors used as crew in theatres in 17th century London.

Drapes   Any soft fabric used to mask or disguise areas of the stage or presentation area.

Genie, or cracked oil, or smoke gun   A machine that creates a mist or fog on stage, to create atmosphere.

Green room   A backstage room for presenters or speakers to wait or relax in.

Ground agent   Someone with local knowledge, who may be a logistics biased expert or technical expert.

Heads up   A theatrical expression used to warn people of movement above their heads – it usually indicates that they should move. It is also used to warn people of changes or items that need their attention, generally in meetings or on communications.

Holding slide   *see* 'Bumper slide'.

Housekeeping   Instructions giving important instructions or information to delegates on eating arrangements, travel, check-out and other similar business.

In charge or in cost   This is the actual cost that a supplier charges before any commission or mark up.

Job bag   The file or files that relate to the job or event. Also refers to the final file after the event has finished.

Lectern   The stand or podium where the speakers make their presentations. There may be more than one lecturn on the stage or platform.

Load in   The unloading of any equipment, staging and scenic elements required for the event.

Load out   Dismantling the set and all the technical equipment and removing it from the venue.

Logo   A term used to refer to the client's or event's symbol or identifying mark or crest.

Logistics   *see* job description of logistics manager. This term may also be used to include transport, and the movement of goods.

Merchandizing   Goods that are sold at the event that are relevant to the event, such as sweat shirts, programmes, and souvenirs.

Mission control   A term used on site to indicate the area where most of the operators, sound, lights, and the show caller are situated.

Mood board   Also referred to as 'tear sheets'. May be used during presentations to the client to show elements of the event in colour, texture or as 'lifestyle' visuals.

Name slide   A slide or visual with the presenter's name and title. The slide may also have the title of the presentation on it as well.

Non-disclosure agreement   The term used for an agreement made between a company and their suppliers literally to not disclose to any third party any information about an event.

Out charge   A figure with commission added or mark-up cost (*see* in charge).

Passes   A shortened form of 'security pass'. Usually in different colours to denote different areas of an event and restricting the wearer to that area.

Per diems   Literally '**each day**'. A term used for any financial allowance that is paid to crew or people working on event in lieu of on site catering.

Pitch   To pitch for a job, piece of work, event means to compete to win the event or to tender for the event or elements of the event.

Podium   Another term for a lectern, may also refer to the raised staging used underneath to raise the speaker.

Point of sale   A stand or place where you can purchase goods.

Pointer   Used by speakers this can be low-tech, for example a wooden pointer, or hi-tech, such as a laser pen, showing a point of light that people can see.

PowerPoint   A software program that is commonly used as 'speaker support', to display materials to support a speaker's presentation. It may include graphics, pictures, graphs and bullet points.

PR   Public relations – usually responsible for press awareness of an event and for ensuring information is distributed to press.

Presentation   Also called the pitch, where a company, individual or supplier presents their ideas, proposal and budget for the event.

Producer   *see* job description.

Production manager   *see* job description.

Pyrotechnics   Any form of 'firework' used on an event. It may include confetti canons, indoor and outdoor fireworks and anything that requires specialist supplies and handling involving gunpowder or a charge to ignite the effect.

Response to brief   This is part of the presentation and the pitch, meaning the event company's ideas and suggestions in response to the client's brief.

Road show   Usually a small event or presentation or exhibition, that travels around visiting many venues.

Rostra/rostrum   Usually a raised box like structure that can be made of metal or wood. A series of these may be used to construct a stage.

Rigging   The method by which anything is suspended or built above the ground.

Running order   A shortened version of the script for the event or show, showing the order of speakers, videos and other elements with their running times and expected start and finish times.

Show caller   *see* job description.

Show blacks   An expression used to indicate to everyone working on the event or show that they should wear black clothing.

Signage   This can relate to road signs, signs on exhibition stands, signs that inform audience of the location of various structures or information points.

Sign off   Confirmation of approval obtained from the client regarding any aspect of the event.

Sim-Tran   Simultaneous translation

Speaker support   This refers to anything that speakers use to support their presentation.

Stage manager   *see* job description

Staging   This can be used in two different contexts. The 'staging' can mean the choreography of an event where speakers, dancers, performers move or appear. Staging can also refer to the platform of scenic elements that are used on an event.

Story board   A series of visuals or pictures set out in sequence, telling the story of your event or video.

Technical manager   *see* job description.

Theatre style   This refers to the layout of the seating at a venue, usually describing seating arranged in straight lines facing the stage.

To kill   A theatrical expression meaning to lose a light or to turn it off, as in 'kill that'.

Tool box   An information kit that is distributed to the client as a roll-out programme of information.

Transport manager   *see* job description

Treads   Usually a 'set of treads'. This refers to a set of steps used to enable people to access stage or similar. May also be called a 'set of two treads, three treads' etc denoting the number of steps necessary to reach the required height.

Venue   A place where an event may be held.

Walk in   The arrival of the audience, also sometimes referred to as the audience 'load in'.

Weight loading   The weight that the place, venue, or stage can safely withstand without subsidence or collapse. It can also refer to the specific weight that by law, the place or venue can withstand.

Wings   The sides of the stage or performance area, usually hidden from the audience.

ADDITIONAL INFORMATION

ABTT (Association of British Theatre Technicians)
47 Bermondsey Street
London
SE1 3XT
Tel: 0207 403 6655
www.abtt.co.uk

National Outdoor Events Association
7 Hamilton Way
Wallington
Surrey
SM6 9NJ
Tel: 0208 669 8121
www.noea.org.uk

TESA (The Event Services Association)
Centre Court
1301 Stratford Road
Hall Green
Birmingham
B28 9HH
Tel: 0121 693 7126
www.tesa.org.uk

The Stage Management Association
55 Farringdon Road
London
EC1M 3JB
Tel: 0207 242 9250
www.stagemanagementassociation.co.uk

PUBLICATIONS

Hal Leonard, *Tour America* (out of print)
(www.amazon.com)

The Guide to Unique Venues
(www.amazon.com)

The White Book
(Entertainment services, equipment and venues)
Tel: 02476 559590
www.whitebook.co.uk

Access all Areas
(Monthly trade publication)
www.access-aa.co.uk

The Event Safety Guide. A Guide to Health and Safety and Welfare at Music and Similar Events
(also called the purple guide).
Health and Safety Executive
ISBN 0 717 62453 6
www.hse.gov.uk

National Outdoor Events Association
Code of Practice for Outdoor Events
Produced by NOEA

Five Steps to Risk Assessment
Health and Safety Executive (HSE)
ISBN 0 717 61565 0
www.hse.gov.uk

ADDITIONAL INFORMATION

Guide to Safety at Sports Grounds
The Stationery Office Books
ISBN 0 113 00095 2
www.hse.gov.uk

Managing Crowds Safely
Health and Safety Executive
ISBN 0 717 61180 9
www.hse.gov.uk

*Safe Operation of Passenger Carrying
Amusement Devices*
(includes bouncy castles)
Health and Safety Executive
ISBN 0 118 85604 9
www.hse.gov.uk

*A Guide to Safety for Fireworks Display
Organisers*
Health and Safety Executive
ISBN 0 717 60835 2
www.hse.gov.uk

INDEX